Minority and Indigenous Trends 2019

Focus on climate justice

Cover: Martha Akal, a Turkana mother of three children, herds her goats in the village of Kache Imeri, Northern Kenya, in the midst of a severe drought. In the absence of safe drinking water and food, pastoralists are extremely vulnerable to disease and famine. Panos / *Frederic Courbet.*

Inside front cover: An elderly Tibetan nomad tends to her yak. Panos / *Kieran Dodds*

Inside back cover: Portrait of a local elderly Amazigh man at Assaiss market in Taliouine, Morocco. Alamy / *Chris Griffiths*

Acknowledgements

Minority Rights Group International (MRG) gratefully acknowledges the support of all organizations and individuals who gave financial and other assistance to this publication, including the European Union.

© Minority Rights Group International, June 2019. All rights reserved.

Material from this publication may be reproduced for teaching or other non-commercial purposes. No part of it may be reproduced in any form for commercial purposes without the prior express permission of the copyright holders.

For further information please contact MRG. A CIP catalogue record of this publication is available from the British Library.

ISBN 978-1-912938-15-5

Published: June 2019

Lead reviewer: Carl Soderbergh
Production: Samrawit Gougsa
Copy editing: Sophie Richmond
Proof reading: Jacqui Lewis
Design: Lucia Rusinakova
With thanks to Tero Mustonen (Snowchange) for his review of the final report. All responsibility for the content of the publication rests with MRG.

Minority Rights Group International
54 Commercial Street
London E1 6LT,
United Kingdom.

Tel: +44 (0)20 7422 4200
Fax: +44 (0)20 7422 4201

Email: minority.rights@mrgmail.org
Website: www.minorityrights.org

Support our work

**Donate at
www.minorityrights.org/donate**
MRG relies on the generous support of institutions and individuals to help us secure the rights of minorities and indigenous peoples around the world. All donations received contribute directly to our projects with minorities and indigenous peoples.

**Read more of our reports at
www.minorityrights.org/publications**
Our publications offer a compelling analysis of minority and indigenous issues and original research. We also offer specialist training materials and guides on international human rights instruments and accessing international bodies.

**Learn more about minority
and indigenous communities
at www.minorityrights.org/directory**
Visit our online directory for country profiles of minorities and indigenous communities around the world.

Follow us:
🐦 @minorityrights
📘 @minorityrights
📷 @minorityrightsgroup

This publication is funded by the European Union. This content is the sole responsibility of Minority Rights Group International and can under no circumstances be regarded as reflecting the position of the European Union.

Minority and Indigenous Trends 2019

Focus on climate justice

Edited by Peter Grant

Minority Rights Group International

Table of Contents

More than half

The northern section of the Great Barrier Reef had already lost more than half of its coral cover since 2016.

90%

Lake Chad has shrunk by an estimated 90 per cent since the 1960s, disrupting the routes and grazing patterns of livestock farmers from the countries around the lake.

24%

The proportion of all carbon stored aboveground in rainforests being managed by indigenous and local communities – amounting to some 54,546 million metric tonnes of carbon (MtC).

Rights and Resources Initiative, Toward a Global Baseline of Carbon Storage in Collective Lands, 2016

Twice as fast

The Arctic is warming twice as fast as anywhere else on earth.

33x higher

The chance of being displaced by wildfires for people living in First Nations reserves over the last 30 years, compared to people living off-reserve.

Todd Kuiack, the Emergency Management Director of Indigenous Services Canada, in Yumagulova, L., 'Community resilience: connecting emergency management, education, infrastructure and economic development', Haznet 10(1), 2018.

425 teragrams

The amount of carbon that forest areas in South America, Africa and Asia are now releasing every year due to logging and degradation – more than the total emissions from traffic in the United States.

Baccini, A. et al, 'Tropical forests are a net carbon source based on aboveground measurements of gain and loss', Science 358(6360), October 2017.

100+

The number of languages spoken in Vanuatu, amounting to the highest per capita of any country in the world. This precious heritage could be threatened by climate change.

2x

Illegal land seizures reached 12 square km in the first three months of 2019 – double the area taken over the same period in 2018.

Data from indigenous NGO Imazon in Pará, Brazil, cited by Amnesty International.

56% and 63% higher

The average levels of exposure to $PM_{2.5}$ pollution among African Americans and Hispanics in the United States, compared to 17 per cent less among non-Hispanic white populations.

Tessum, C. et al., 'Inequity in consumption of goods and services adds to racial–ethnic disparities in air pollution exposure', PNAS 116(13), March 2019.

Foreword

Joshua Castellino,
Executive Director of Minority Rights Group International

For many climate change is a terrifying prospect in the near future, a threat that could soon bring incalculable catastrophe to our lives. For others, however, this disaster has already begun. From melting ice in the Arctic to rising sea levels in the Pacific, from droughts in the Sahel to shrinking coral reefs in Australia, minorities and indigenous peoples are on the front line of environmental collapse. The cost to humanity could prove immense: the devastation of entire communities and their way of life. This new report by Minority Rights Group International is a timely reminder of how much we all stand to lose if we choose not to act.

The challenges, of course, go beyond the immediate environmental issues, overwhelming though these may be, and reflect the wider social, political and economic realities of our world today. As we know, disasters discriminate. Minorities, indigenous peoples and other marginalized groups such as women, children and persons with disabilities are all typically the worst affected. Besides being more exposed to shocks such as storms and flooding, they may also lack the necessary resources to recover - particularly when authorities themselves may be guilty of discriminating against them when delivering post-disaster emergency relief.

Too often, discussion around climate change overlooks this dimension of discrimination. We certainly need to invest significantly in the right infrastructure and technologies, including renewable energy, to help us transition to a more sustainable future. But if human rights are not at the heart of this process, we are doomed to fail. As documented in this report, indigenous communities such as Kenya's Sengwer have suffered brutal evictions in the name of adaptation and conservation. In these instances, minority and indigenous communities which have sustainably stewarded forests, lakes and rivers for generations have been left even more vulnerable to climate change and other pressures.

On one level, this makes our present predicament even more daunting. The barriers we face are not only the steadily accumulating crises of a wounded biosphere, but also the deep-rooted hierarchies that place minorities, indigenous peoples and other groups at the bottom of almost every society. For them, climate justice is the latest chapter in a long history of exclusion. Until that story is rewritten and the continuing impact of racism and discrimination is reversed, there can be no true and lasting solutions to climate change.

But there is also reason for hope. To respond decisively to climate change, we must also lay the foundations for a fairer world. A world where rainforests are protected, fossil fuel consumption is reduced and everyone is able to access the support they need to survive environmental shocks is also, by definition, one where indigenous land rights are respected and discrimination against minorities no longer exists. As this publication demonstrates, despite the many barriers and the continued violence, poverty and exclusion communities face, there are activists and campaigners working hard to make this dream a reality. For all our sakes, we need to do everything we can to ensure they succeed.

Executive summary

Climate change poses a profound environmental challenge that will leave no country or community untouched. Its social impact, if unaddressed, will reinforce inequalities, deepen poverty and leave the world's most marginalized populations in greater insecurity. Minorities and indigenous peoples are already living with its consequences, from rising sea levels and higher temperatures to increasingly frequent extreme weather events such as severe storms. Their isolation and exclusion in many countries leave them disproportionately exposed to these negative effects.

Discrimination frequently dictates the ways that members of these communities experience shocks. There is now increased recognition that 'natural' disasters are often social and institutional in character too. Excluded populations such as South Asia's Dalits, for instance, are frequently concentrated in areas like Dhaka's flood-prone 'colonies', where lack of access to water and sanitation leaves residents more vulnerable during monsoons. They may also be side-lined from emergency assistance in the aftermath due to discrimination. Their stigmatization is therefore replicated at every stage and may be exacerbated further in the event of displacement, loss of income or illness.

While vulnerability may reflect a more general lack of resources to invest adequately in adaptation measures, this is by no means the whole picture. Even in more affluent countries like the United States (US), broader societal inequalities translate into uneven outcomes among different groups. The most widely cited example of this is the devastation wrought by Hurricane Katrina in New Orleans in 2005 with its disproportionate impact on victims belonging to minorities, particularly African Americans. Similar disparities have played out in the wake of subsequent disasters since, including Hurricane Sandy in coastal New Jersey in 2012 and Hurricane Maria in Puerto Rico in 2017, with minorities worst affected.

It is nevertheless the case that many communities, especially indigenous peoples, have long lived in pristine or fragile ecosystems that are uniquely sensitive to the effects of a changing climate. In the Arctic region, where temperatures are rising twice as fast as the rest of the planet, Sámi and other indigenous communities are struggling to adapt, as melting ice and other impacts threaten traditional livelihoods such as reindeer herding. In this instance, climate change is one element in a wider context where both human rights and the environment are under threat as a result of industrial development and the encroachment of activities such as mining on their territories.

Many aspects of the relationship between climate change and migration remain under-explored by researchers and are largely unacknowledged by governments, notwithstanding recent initiatives such as the 2018 Global Compact for Safe, Orderly and Regular Migration. It is clear that environmental stresses intersect in many cases with social, economic and political considerations to increase migration, be it voluntary or forced, from rural areas to cities and even across national borders. It seems likely, for instance, that for some Central American migrants, the decision to head north towards the US may be driven not only by a desire for a better life and the need to escape violence in their home countries, but also due to negative climate impacts on agriculture and other traditional income sources.

For pastoralists in sub-Saharan Africa, the ability to migrate to maintain their nomadic way of life is increasingly constrained by a range of factors, including desertification, drought and reduced rainfall. In Chad, one of the countries most vulnerable to climate change, changing weather patterns and increased pressure on water and land for grazing has disrupted traditional migration routes and exacerbated conflict with sedentary communities as competition for resources has intensified. These tensions reflect a long history of intercommunal division and discrimination, though Chad has taken steps to reduce these threats through efforts to develop better managed migration routes by engaging pastoralists themselves.

The Pacific is another area where the link between climate change and migration – already widespread among many indigenous communities due to the lack of economic opportunities in their countries – has become chronic. For low-lying islands such as Kiribati, rising sea levels pose an existential threat to a wealth of cultural and spiritual traditions tied inextricably to their homelands. Faced with the prospect of its territory becoming uninhabitable, the government has been planning the resettlement of much of its population. Even if these countries are able to avert a humanitarian catastrophe in the decades to come, their unique heritage could face extinction.

Besides the incalculable loss to the communities affected, the erosion of traditional practices and indigenous knowledge systems represents a major blow to global efforts to respond effectively to climate change. Across the world, indigenous peoples' unique understanding of local ecosystems and their ability to identify, manage and respond to environmental fluctuations, developed over centuries, has enabled communities to live sustainably off forests, lakes, rivers and seas while developing resilience to flooding, drought and other shocks. Approximately 80 per cent of the world's remaining biodiversity is stewarded by indigenous peoples – a situation that would logically justify their place at the centre of environmental decision-making.

Though there is increasing recognition of the value of traditional knowledge in combating climate change, including concerted efforts from scientific and governmental bodies to incorporate this learning, indigenous peoples continue to play a marginal role in international policy. As a corollary, the commodification of indigenous knowledge without consideration of the wider rights of those communities leaves indigenous peoples vulnerable to intellectual property theft and other violations. This reflects a broader problem of power inequalities that has left minority and indigenous communities on the fringes of national and international negotiations around climate change. This travesty is heightened by the fact that these communities are among those least responsible for its causes, but worst affected by its consequences.

This is especially evident when it comes to land rights and the continued threat posed by mining, plantations, logging and other commercially oriented developments. These activities undermine every aspect of their lives and wellbeing, from food security to health, and weaken their ability to respond to climate change and other environmental pressures. In many cases, the situation is exacerbated by top-down programmes undertaken in the name of 'green' energy and climate change mitigation. In the Brazilian Amazon, for instance, indigenous communities face displacement and flooding following the construction of hydroelectric dams such as Belo Monte without their free, prior and informed consent. Besides the damage inflicted on local communities, with thousands of lives uprooted, the supposed environmental benefits of these developments are increasingly being called into question. Conservation has been used as a pretext to force communities from their ancestral lands. This is the case for Kenya's Sengwer people who, despite living in the Embobut Forest for centuries, have been violently evicted by Kenya Forest Service guards with connections to environmental and climate change programmes funded by international donors such as the European Union and the World Bank.

Examples such as these demonstrate how immediate climate change impacts intersect with a range of other environmental rights issues, from fossil fuel extraction to exposure to pollution. While environmental harm caused by fossil fuel extraction is often thought of as a different issue, both the processes involved and the uses to which the fossil fuel is put are major drivers of global warming. Much fossil fuel extraction takes place on communal lands. As a result, indigenous protests around land rights such as the Standing Rock demonstrations in the US now increasingly align with climate change activism. Similarly, though air pollution in cities may be primarily attributed to the immediate effects of fossil fuel consumption rather than long-term climate change impacts, it is likely both to contribute to climate change and be exacerbated by it. With a number of recent studies suggesting that minorities are on average more exposed to air pollution, this signals how closely the issue is tied to a climate justice perspective.

Ultimately, the vulnerability of minorities, indigenous peoples and other excluded groups including women, children, LGBTQ+ people and people with disabilities to climate change is a product of a wider backdrop of discrimination, encompassing land, housing, culture, livelihoods and migration. The surest means of strengthening communities' resilience is through protection of their fundamental rights to effective participation, identity, land, livelihoods and human security. Such an approach could transform communities from victims of climate change impacts to leaders of adaptation – a situation that would not only support the development of a more equitable global society, but also enhance the abilities of humanity as a whole in adapting to the current climate crisis.

RECOMMENDATIONS

HUMAN RIGHTS AND CLIMATE JUSTICE

- *Mainstream minority and indigenous rights into national and international climate change strategies:* this requires clear recognition of the rights of minorities and indigenous peoples, particularly to their lands as well as traditional occupations and livelihoods, with guarantees to full and effective participation and consent. Governments should also integrate climate change considerations into national development plans, including progress towards the Sustainable Development Goals (SDGs), and addressing the specific concerns of minority and indigenous communities.

- *Establish clear mechanisms to monitor and assess climate change-related impacts affecting minorities and indigenous peoples:* this should include a particular focus on women, children, LGBTQ+ people, people with disabilities and other groups who face intersectional discrimination on account of their minority or indigenous identity. Governments should also take concrete steps to prevent inequitable or exclusionary climate aid and relief through disaggregated indicators on the delivery of emergency assistance, resilience strengthening and other forms of support.

- *Situate climate policies in a broader framework of minority and indigenous rights that addresses the root causes of inequality and increased vulnerability among these communities:* as impacts from climate change intersect indirectly with a range of other social, political and institutional factors, authorities should develop a holistic approach rooted in concepts of climate justice. This includes improving access to water, sanitation and waste management services, providing official recognition and protection to customary land rights, regularizing land tenure in informal settlements, livelihood diversification, improved health care and education.

POLITICAL PARTICIPATION

■ *Enable minorities and indigenous peoples to engage fully and equitably in climate governance and policy development at a national and international level:* in particular, established global climate bodies such as the United Nations Framework Convention on Climate Change (UNFCCC) and other agencies should establish mechanisms for communities to participate meaningfully in negotiations. At a country level, governments should establish dedicated platforms to ensure their voices are heard to promote locally driven, community-led solutions.

TRADITIONAL KNOWLEDGE

■ *Recognize the rights of minorities and indigenous peoples as custodians of their traditions and protect this heritage from expropriation by governments, businesses and other groups:* while growing interest in traditional knowledge and its application to climate adaptation strategies is welcome, this must be in line with the right of minorities to meaningful participation and the right of indigenous peoples to free, prior and informed consent (FPIC) with respect for their right to maintain their lands, resources and intellectual property.

■ *Support the integration of traditional practices and knowledge systems into adaptation strategies, within a clear rights-based framework*: international bodies, governments and other actors should make concerted efforts to ensure that minorities and indigenous peoples are able to communicate their knowledge and perspectives into decision-making processes, particularly those affecting them at a local level. This should include mandatory reporting in the nationally determined contributions (NDCs) of signatory states to the 2015 Paris Agreement on the use of traditional knowledge in their adaptation strategies.

LAND RIGHTS

■ *Enforce the right of minorities and indigenous peoples to their lands and the protection of territories from development projects, including those threatening to exacerbate climate change:* oil extraction, logging and mining are all acknowledged threats to local communities that also, through excavation of more fossil fuels or the release of carbon stored in forests, contribute to climate change.

■ *Ensure any environmental or conservation programmes are designed and implemented within clear rights-based frameworks for any communities affected:* for example, the risks posed by hydroelectric dam construction, the creation of national parks without consultation on minority and indigenous lands and other supposedly 'green' initiatives to communities should be recognized and any developments that violate these rights immediately suspended.

■ *Strengthen international solidarity mechanisms, including funding and other forms of support, for the most climate vulnerable countries:* in particular, governments should provide significant resources to Pacific island states at risk of inundation from rising sea levels to enable them, as much as possible, to remain in their territories if they so wish. While options to migrate voluntarily to other countries should be facilitated for residents of affected areas who wish to do so as a coping strategy, efforts should also be made to support those who wish to stay in their homes through resilience building.

MIGRATION

■ *Develop a better understanding and recognition of the linkages between climate change and migration, both internally and internationally:* despite some acknowledgement in the Global Compact for Safe, Orderly and Regular Migration, governments remain reluctant to acknowledge the potential role of climate change as a driver of human mobility, particularly in the case of refugees and asylum seekers. This is in part a reflection of the lack of research in this area and the need to address these information gaps.

INTERCOMMUNAL CONFLICT

■ *Take concrete steps to anticipate and resolve increasing resource shortages to reduce intercommunal conflict, particularly between pastoralist and sedentary communities:* in regions where grazing land and water are becoming increasingly scarce, raising the possibility of violent conflict between nomadic herders and local farmers, authorities need to bring all parties together and negotiate accepted agreements around migration routes and timings to resolve tensions.

Thematic Chapters

Minorities and Indigenous Peoples in an Age of Climate Change

Helle Abelvik-Lawson, Mariam Kizilbash, Joanna James and Damien Short

While much of the policy and media discussion around climate change focuses on future projections, minorities and indigenous peoples across the world are already living with some of its most challenging impacts. This is a reflection not only of their relative social, economic and political marginalization, but also the close connection of many communities with their land and their dependence on local resources for their physical and cultural survival.

Given their long-standing socio-economic disadvantages and a high capacity for sustainable environmental stewardship – an estimated 80 per cent of the planet's remaining biodiversity is cared for by indigenous peoples[1] – they are also the least responsible for climate change.

Despite this, they have been largely sidelined from policy discussions and decision-making at an international level. The 1992 United Nations Framework Convention on Climate Change (UNFCCC) and its 1997 Kyoto Protocol, for instance, while seen as important forums to present key issues of justice and human rights alongside international climate policy, made no mention of minorities or indigenous peoples.[2] The situation has improved to some extent in

---

1   https://unfccc.int/news/indigenous-empowerment-is-vital-for-climate-action
2   UN General Assembly, United Nations Framework Convention on Climate Change: Resolution / adopted by the General Assembly, 20 January 1994, A/RES/48/189; Kyoto Protocol to the United Nations Framework Convention on Climate Change, Dec. 10, 1997, U.N. Doc FCCC/CP/1997/7/ Add.1, 37 I.L.M. 22 (1998).

recent years, with many minority and indigenous activists working hard to engage with UN climate negotiations: encouragingly, the preamble to the Paris Agreement 2015 specifically mentions the rights of indigenous peoples while noting that climate change is a common concern of humankind.

While uncertainties remain about the different possible scenarios that climate change will bring, with our ability to respond now to address its causes and impacts playing an important role in this, the effects will undoubtedly be severe and wide-ranging in many parts of the world, with higher temperatures, unpredictable rainfall and a host of knock-on effects. This chapter explores the ways climate change will play out in different contexts across the world, with reference to the broader context of minorities and indigenous peoples. Among other areas, it looks at:

- *The role of discrimination in increasing vulnerability to climate change impacts,* with reference to the exposure of Dalit communities in Bangladesh and India to flooding and their exclusion from official disaster response mechanisms, as well as the impacts of storms and hurricanes on minority and indigenous communities in the United States (US) and Caribbean.
- *Ecological fragility, livelihoods and development,* exploring how climate change threatens to undermine traditional herding among Arctic communities, while 'green' programmes such as dam construction in the Brazilian Amazon are causing further problems for indigenous populations.
- *Traditional knowledge and the threat of cultural extinction,* drawing out some of the pressures and adaptive responses to climate change pursued by

indigenous Pacific Islanders in the face of rising sea levels.
- *Land rights and the threat of evictions,* focusing on the situation of Uganda's Batwa and how their long history of discrimination, particularly their removal from their ancestral land in the Bwindi Forest, has left them more exposed to food insecurity, poor health and other impacts connected in part to climate change.
- *Migration as a consequence of climate change,* with a brief overview of the role environmental stress may be playing in driving migration from Central America to the US.

Ultimately, the vulnerability of minorities, indigenous peoples and other marginalized groups including women, children, elderly people and people with disabilities to climate change is also a reflection of a much broader context of discrimination, spanning land, housing, culture, livelihoods and migration. A central element in improving the resilience of these groups depends on the willingness of governments, businesses and other actors to fully respect these rights.

Increased vulnerability as a result of social exclusion

Minorities and indigenous peoples are typically more vulnerable to the impacts of climate change than majority populations due to a range of factors. For minorities, these can include extreme relative poverty and their location in peripheral or degraded urban areas that are disproportionately exposed to extreme weather and heat. This begins with their location, with minorities and indigenous peoples often concentrated in regions that are especially exposed to climate change impacts such as higher temperatures, rising sea levels and flooding. This may be in part because of the location of their settlements in naturally risk-prone places such as riverbanks and vulnerable coastlines, but may also be a reflection of the social marginalization of the areas they reside in – a location near an environmentally hazardous landfill site, for instance, or an informal settlement without basic services such as sanitation and waste management. This can leave them not only more exposed to the impacts of an extreme weather event but also less able to recover from the shocks.

For many members of minorities, particularly the most marginalized groups within them, the environmental burden of climate change is exacerbated by social inequalities. Consequently, one of the most effective means to address climate change is to support the resilience of high-risk groups such as minorities, indigenous peoples and the poor through rights-based policies to land, services and other basic needs. Unfortunately, government responses to climate change impacts can often exacerbate the situation for poorer populations. In Jakarta, for instance, the world's fastest 'sinking' city, colonial-era Kampung settlements – urban villages where land tenure is irregular – are now frequently cleared as part of Jakarta's 'river normalization' programme, developed with technical expertise from the Netherlands. This example illustrates how top-down, technocratic responses to climate change can, without adequate consultation and respect for human rights, compound the problems of environmental stress for poor and marginalized communities.

The role that social discrimination can play in deepening vulnerability to climate change is typically felt at every stage of a disaster, with marginalized groups not only more exposed to these impacts but also frequently overlooked by authorities in the aftermath. Government recovery and preventative measures can overlook minority or indigenous communities and their lack of resettlement options and resources. Following a storm, those who are forced to move may even be unable to return to their coastal homes and traditional livelihoods as a result of government policies. This dynamic was apparent in the Philippines following Typhoon Haiyan, known locally as Yolanda, where authorities earmarked the land customarily occupied by fisher folk as the 'Salvage Zone'. This prohibited the construction of any private structures, effectively evicting the displaced groups from their homes, without funding for appropriate replacement housing – a policy that left those affected in an even more precarious situation.

Other barriers to inclusive adaptation and resilience include language: linguistic minorities may suffer as a result of being unable to access technical information and warnings about extreme weather events. In Australia, for example, members of indigenous communities in the Northern Territory were unprepared for the impacts of Tropical Cyclone Trevor in March 2019, as information about the path of the cyclone was only provided in English. Hundreds self-evacuated as the cyclone made landfall, unable to understand the updated information from the Bureau of Meteorology that suggested their town would remain unscathed. Any information that was translated was related to health warnings, such as to boil water before consuming it, but the translations did not extend to the path of the storm or predictions of the places that would be most affected.

Flooding in South Asia:
Pre-existing discrimination
leaves Dalit communities
more vulnerable to shocks

Across South Asia, Dalit communities frequently reside in the least hospitable environments in urban and rural areas, including forests, and are often among the worst affected by environmental shocks. Yet the present institutional mechanisms for disaster management generally do not recognize these vulnerabilities, meaning that the immediate impacts of a disaster may be exacerbated by institutional neglect.

Many Dalits in Bangladesh and India live in the heavily populated urban areas of the coastal Bay of Bengal region, the largest bay in the world. Dalits have faced the triple pressures of discrimination, severe poverty and environmental stress for centuries. These vulnerabilities are set to deepen with climate change, however, with Dalits further disadvantaged by a lack of equity in adaptation and mitigation response.

Because of its geography, Bangladesh is widely considered to be one of the countries in the world most vulnerable to climate change. Climate change in this region is expected to continue to cause accelerating cyclones, inland and coastal flooding, low water levels and drought, salinization of fresh-water supplies and riverbank erosion. This will in turn have impacts on the food security of Dalits, who depend on fish from the Bay of Bengal and crops from coastal land areas. Although impacts are accelerating, they are not new: a long-term flood in 1988 prevented farmers from planting their crops in time, leading to a 45 per cent loss in production. Further unexpected weather changes in future will reduce the availability of subsistence and land-based resources for rural Dalits in Bangladesh.[3]

The continued movement towards urban areas of rural Bangladeshis is particularly concerning, due to the strain put on coastal cities like Dhaka, which are themselves suffering from rising waters and difficulty recovering from extreme monsoon seasons. With as many as 400,000 migrants arriving in Dhaka every year, many of whom are driven in part by environmental shocks in the countryside, the city – already prone to frequent flooding – must now contend with the effects of a warming climate, with rising sea levels and melting Himalayan glaciers likely to expose vulnerable areas to even greater risks. The impacts are likely to impact on Dhaka's most marginalized populations, such as Dalits, who make up many of the poorest slum dwellers in the city's 'sweeper colonies', so-called because many residents are employed as waste pickers. Government evictions from these colonies are common, and for Dalits there are few protections from discrimination. While there are few detailed studies on these vulnerable communities, there are known water and sanitation risks to Dalit communities in Dhaka due to the city's high flood risks, a vulnerability that will continue to increase as the climate crisis escalates.

It is not only in Dhaka that floods are an issue for Dalit communities. Following flooding in 2015 in Chennai, the capital of India's Tamil Nadu state, Dalit families were worst hit but were reportedly neglected during relief efforts. Furthermore, the burden of cleaning the city once floodwaters receded fell to Dalits, who are typically engaged in janitorial labour. Thousands of Dalit workers were mobilized from around

---

3   Sugden, F., de Silva, S., Clement, F., Maskey-Amatya, N., Ramesh, V., Philip, A. and Bharati, L.,
     *A Framework to Understand Gender and Structural Vulnerability to Climate Change in the Ganges
     River Basin: Lessons from Bangladesh, India and Nepal*, IMWI Working Paper 159, 2014, p. 3.

the state for the month-long clean-up operation. Handling 8,000 to 10,000 tons of garbage every day during the floods, containing mixed materials including electric and medical waste, a vast majority of Dalit janitors faced both the stigma of caste and 'dirty work', with continued job and economic insecurity and little access to health care and employment benefits.[4]

Dalit women are particularly vulnerable to climate impacts due to intersectional discrimination on the basis of gender as well as caste. Systemic discrimination propagated by the Hindu caste system has prevented most Dalits from owning property, with the large majority of Dalit farmers in Tamil Nadu engaged as landless labourers. The situation is even more acute, however, for Dalit women given the gender imbalances in land ownership – women comprise less than 14 per cent of agricultural land holders in India as a whole – leaving them even more vulnerable to climate change impacts. With established weather patterns increasingly disrupted, communities are now struggling to adapt, with more intense cyclones and unpredictable rainfall patterns that combine periods of heavy rain and drought. In this context, some Dalit women have taken up collective farming to survive, a remarkable step given the deep-seated barriers they face in accessing land. This arrangement offers the possibility of greater security and autonomy in future, but collective members face the challenge not only of inundation, water scarcity and contamination of crops, but also the additional burden of discrimination, including harassment, higher rents and other exclusionary practices.[5]

North America and the Caribbean: Minorities and indigenous peoples continue to be excluded in the wake of natural disasters
Though many developing countries may struggle to raise sufficient resources to invest in effective adaptation strategies, the situation in many developed countries also illustrates that, in contexts of inequality, certain groups may still be disproportionately affected. Relief and recovery efforts can also disadvantage urban minorities and coastal indigenous communities, who may receive less assistance than the majority population. Earlier disasters in the US, like Hurricane Katrina in 2005, had huge negative effects on minorities living in and around New Orleans compared to the white population.

In the US, the threat of sea-level rises and storms is particularly stark for coastal indigenous communities and socio-economically vulnerable ethnic minorities. In Louisiana, where land has been lost steadily to the sea, the Isle de Jean Charles, in the bayous of the Delta, has reduced from 22,400 acres to 320 due to a combination of rising water, erosion, subsidence and a series of hurricanes, including Hurricane Katrina in 2007 and Hurricane Isaac in 2012. The Band of Biloxi-Chitimacha-Choctaw, who have lived on the island for two centuries, are now being relocated to safer ground as part of a government-brokered resettlement programme. Yet the process has itself proved acrimonious as tribal leaders have accused the authorities of sidelining them from the process and failing to respect their rights to continued autonomy over the land.

4   Mahalingam, R., Jagannathan, S. and Selvaraj, P., 'Decasticization, dignity, and "dirty work" at the intersections of caste, memory, and disaster', *Business Ethics Quarterly* 29(2), April 2019, pp. 213–39.
5   Kolachalam, N., '"Caste, the patriarchy, and climate change', *Slate*, 15 February 2019.

A young girl is carried by her father in the Astrodome stadium in Houston, Texas, where refugees received food and shelter following Hurricane Katrina.

Reuters / *Carlos Barria*

Other disasters in the US have illustrated that, despite the country's wealth and resources, environmental shocks can still have severe impacts on minorities, indigenous peoples and other groups with limited power or resources. Research has shown that, in the aftermath of Hurricane Sandy's passage of destruction through central and coastal New Jersey in 2012, ethnic minorities went for a longer period as evacuees, without power or heat. Furthermore, Hispanic residents had more acute health care needs and lacked access to medical care centres serving those without insurance.[6] Age, disability and gender are also important factors dictating the effect of natural disasters on marginal groups: the average age among the victims of Sandy, for instance, was around 60 years old.[7]

A similar picture emerges in Puerto Rico in the wake of Hurricane Maria in 2017, where the median age of adults who stayed behind or died was 50 years old and mortality rates were highest for the oldest, poorest residents. An 'unincorporated territory' of the US, with no voting member in the US Congress, Puerto Rico is populated mainly by Hispanic, mixed-race and other minority groups. In the aftermath of the storm it appeared that Puerto Rico was neglected by the US federal government, which failed to offer adequate aid and assistance. Anger in Puerto Rico at the slow response from the central government

6   Burger, J., Gochfeld, M., Pittfield, T. and Jeitner, C., 'Responses of a vulnerable Hispanic population in New Jersey to Hurricane Sandy: Access to care, medical needs, concerns, and ecological ratings', *Journal of Toxicology and Environmental Health, Part A* 80(6), March 2017, pp. 315–25.
7   Centers for Disease Control and Prevention, 'Deaths associated with Hurricane Sandy: October–November 2012', 24 May 2013.

was further inflamed when mayor of San Juan and other officials were attacked by President Donald Trump in early 2019 as 'incompetent or corrupt', while still being denied appropriate funds to remedy the situation.

Hurricane Maria also left significant damage on Dominica, a Caribbean island with a population of just over 70,000. Dominica was particularly hard hit by Hurricane Maria on 18 September 2017. Its Kalinago population, at around 3,000-strong, is now the largest group of indigenous people in the East Caribbean; they live on communally owned land, making a living from forest products and handicrafts. However, their territory took a direct hit from Hurricane Maria, cutting off all communications and creating serious water shortages. Furthermore, their geographic location meant that aid was slow to reach the area. Indeed, new reports suggested that food, water and other supplies that were earmarked for the region never made it out of Roseau, Dominica's capital city. Though community rebuilding efforts were supported by faith groups, foreign funds and local private sector companies, these were hampered by the general lack of availability of materials in Dominica; these had to be sourced from nearby St Lucia. However, building standards were raised as a result, diminishing concerns that repeat storms within the 2018 season would cause as much damage. This suggests that the government has tried to use the experience of Hurricane Maria to build greater climate impact resilience: for example, officials and Kalinago community members have worked together on disaster preparedness training to assess failures and improve future responses. While Dominica's recovery was constrained by underdevelopment at a national

level and a relatively small amount of available funding, there was at least clear leadership on resilience-building and efforts to reduce the Kalinago community's vulnerabilities – a striking contrast to the Trump administration's response to Puerto Rico.

Ecological fragility, livelihoods and development

The reliance of many minority and indigenous communities on local resources such as lakes and forests leaves them vulnerable to loss of livelihoods as a result of climate change, as flooding, droughts and wildfires place increasing pressure on scarce water, land and food. This is particularly the case for those situated in fragile environments, such as the Amazon or the Arctic, where environmental shifts, combined with other factors such as pollution and illegal logging, have complex and wide ranging effects on communities' ability to maintain their traditional livelihoods. This predicament is exacerbated by the fact that, when development is brought into their areas, minority and indigenous residents are often left worse off than before. In Colombia, for example, the world's second-largest cultivator of sugarcane after Brazil, minority Afro-Colombian communities in the area surrounding Cali, in the coastal state of Valle de Cauca, have seen their traditional farming practices threatened by the increasing presence of the sugarcane industry. The arrival of large-scale agriculture, while undermining the sustainability of smallholdings, has done little to address the high levels of poverty and unemployment in the area.

Across the world, communities are also struggling against multilateral attempts to offset carbon emissions and seek low-carbon energy alternatives to global energy markets. Ancestral lands and traditional livelihoods are under threat from schemes such as mega-agrofuel cultivation, the establishment of large windfarms, the mining of rare minerals for batteries, hydroelectric dam building in tropical rainforest areas and international climate schemes for 'clean development' and forest conservation. In addition, many indigenous and minority communities continue to suffer from the common encroachments of fossil fuel extraction, in some places made more accessible by climate impacts. For example, communities in the Arctic are fighting against both a warming environment and ongoing plans to drill for or transport oil through the formerly impassable frozen Arctic.

One major global forest conservation scheme, the UN Programme on Reducing Emissions from Deforestation and Forest Degradation (REDD+), has been accused by critics of undermining community land rights and causing conflict among numerous indigenous communities in sub-Saharan Africa and Latin America.[8] Other 'conservation' programmes, some with significant funding from international donors, have also resulted in widespread displacement of communities from their land. One of the most egregious cases in this regard is the situation of Kenya's indigenous Sengwer who, despite living for centuries in the Embobut Forest, have been subjected to repeated evictions by Kenya Forest Service (KFS) guards from their lands, with hundreds of homes burned down and many injured in the process. A number of projects, including a World Bank project and more recently a forest conservation and climate change mitigation programme funded

by the European Union (EU), have been accused of complicity in these abuses. A leaked 2014 report by the World Bank's independent inspection panel revealed that the Sengwer community had written to it after thousands had been evicted from a reserve in the name of forest conservation; the panel accepted that there had been 'a lack of recognition of customary rights' as well as inadequate assessment of the risk that the KFS would engage in forced evictions. In 2018, the EU suspended funding on this project in response to these and other reports. In addition to the trauma of displacement, uprooted Sengwer are also struggling to develop new livelihood opportunities without access to the forest resources on which their livelihoods depended.

Dams, plantations and mining in Latin America: The devastation of indigenous communities by 'green' development

Over the past half century, numerous hydroelectric dam schemes have been constructed in the Brazilian Amazon, flooding hundreds of square kilometres of indigenous territories used for hunting, fishing and the practice of indigenous traditions closely connected to the river and rainforest. Many of these dams are considered 'low carbon', despite being responsible for high levels of dangerous greenhouse gases such as methane – far more warming than CO_2 in the short term – by inundating vast areas of methane-releasing vegetation. Despite their harmful impact, however, these schemes have received funding from the international Clean Development Mechanism (CDM) on the understanding that hydroelectricity is a low-emitting form of energy production, despite the growing body

8   Raftopoulos, M. and Short, D. 'Implementing free prior and informed consent: The United Nations Declaration on the Rights of Indigenous Peoples (2007), the challenges of REDD+ and the case for the precautionary principle', *International Journal of Human Rights*, February 2019.

of evidence on dams in tropical regions suggesting that this is far from true.[9]

The largest and perhaps most infamous, the Belo Monte Dam, started in 2019. The dam and its reservoirs displaced around 20,000 indigenous people from their ancestral lands, including the Kayapó, Juruna, Arara and Xikrin peoples. Plans for hydroelectric dams in another part of the southern Brazilian Amazon, in this case to create a 'soy hydroway' from the south to the Amazon river delta, were shelved in 2016, to the relief of the Munduruku people indigenous to the region. The revival of such projects following the election of President Jair Bolsonaro remains a concern for indigenous communities whose cultural survival and physical existence depends on the river and surrounding forests. Other forms of supposedly 'green' development, such as monoculture for low-carbon fuels, have also devastated indigenous communities in Brazil. In the Brazilian Mato Grosso do Sul, for instance, bio-ethanol fuel producers have uprooted thousands of Kaiowá and Guaraní community members, displacing them from land to which they have rights enshrined in the Brazilian Constitution:[10] some 258 community leaders have been murdered in the state between 2003 and 2011, and there are signs of a growing suicide crisis among indigenous youth in the area.

Similar challenges, including lithium extraction, are also evident elsewhere in Latin America. Global automobile companies are investing in lithium mining to ensure a steady supply of the metal for batteries in their electric car ranges. In the so-called 'Lithium Triangle' of the Andean border regions of Argentina, Bolivia and Chile, lithium miners are encroaching on indigenous territories where salt is traditionally cultivated and harvested to 'mine' water by evaporating lithium-rich brines. Lithium mining is thought by some scientists to lower the water table, causing further problems for communities struggling with drought in the driest region in the world.[11] The growth of this industry also has the potential to contaminate land with the chemicals used to extract lithium from other elements. While this industry is already growing rapidly, the implications of lithium mining are unknown at scale, meaning the transition towards electric cars in the global North will likely have unintended consequences for local indigenous communities.

Higher temperatures in the Arctic: Loss of livelihoods for indigenous reindeer herders and a way of life under threat
The Arctic is warming twice as fast as anywhere else on Earth. As the Arctic's sea-ice melts, the 'albedo' effect of the region's usually high surface-reflectivity is reduced, accelerating heat absorption. Furthermore, there is a high risk of runaway climate change as a result of methane release from under the permafrost in northern Canada and Russia's Siberia. This will have untold consequences for human life in the region and through knock-on impacts on global sea temperatures, and an accompanying impact on the development of extreme weather, such as storms. In this context, northern

9 Deemer, B., Harrison, J., Li, S., Beaulieu, J., DelSontro, T., Barros, N. et al., 'Greenhouse gas emissions from reservoir water surfaces: A new global synthesis', *BioScience* 66(11), November 2016, pp. 949–64.
10 Fois, F. and Machado, S. 'Blood in bio-ethanol: How indigenous peoples' lives are being destroyed by global agribusiness in Brazil', *The Conversation*, 30 August 2018.
11 Abelvik-Lawson, H., *Indigenous Environmental Rights, Participation and Lithium Mining in Argentina and Bolivia: A Socio-legal Analysis*, Doctoral thesis, University of Essex, forthcoming.

indigenous peoples – from Canadian Inuit, Métis and First Nations, to Sámi and Nenets indigenous reindeer herders in the Nordic countries and Russia respectively – are facing the domino effect of loss of livelihoods and associated traditional cultures.

The Sámi indigenous communities of northern Europe are those inhabiting Sápmi, a region encompassing parts of northern Sweden, Norway, Finland and the Kola Peninsula of Russia. Defining who is Sámi for statistical purposes is not always straightforward and often refers to those who either speak or have ancestors who speak Sámi languages. Sámi are spread over a large geographical area and have long engaged in reindeer herding as a livelihood. Although the majority now depend on other forms of livelihood, the practice continues to form a large part of their indigenous identity. Their population is estimated at 20,000 to 40,000 in Sweden, 50,000 to 65,000 in Norway, 8,000 to 10,000 in Finland and 2,000 in Russia.

Arctic air temperatures for the period 2014–18 have exceeded all previous records since 1900. With higher temperatures leading to more rainfall, the snow cover in many areas has become coated in a hard layer of ice. Also, higher warming rates in winter have been recorded, as well as more rain in winter. There has also been less snow, even where winter rain is increasing, and more frequent extreme weather such as storms, alongside coastal erosion, diminishing sea-ice, melting permafrost and acidification. An ice-free Arctic Ocean in the summer is expected within the next two decades. Given the fragile balance at play in the

Arctic ecosystem, there is speculation that climate change impacts could in the long term interact with other factors to trigger even more serious outcomes – for example, the possibility that melting ice sheets in Antarctica and Greenland could result in sea levels rising by dozens of metres in centuries to come.[12]

The implications of these impacts are further complicated by their wide ranging implications for different elements of the local ecosystem, from large predators like lynx, wolverines and brown bears to vegetation. In particular, winter thaws, rain-on-snow and refreezing events are projected to increase, creating ice crust and negatively affecting reindeer pasture conditions, since reindeer cannot dig for their lichen-based nutrition from underneath the layer of hard ice. Climate change also undermines traditional Sámi's reindeer-herding skills and knowledge: increasingly unpredictable weather conditions make it much harder for herders to foresee changes in the way they could previously. It is also important to situate the challenges of climate change in the broader context of marginalization that many Sámi experience, as well as the ways these contribute to poorer health outcomes in certain areas – for example, higher levels of work-related accidents and suicide.[13] As the traditional cultural-ecological framework of the Sámi consists of the *eallu* (the reindeer) and the kinship-based communal structure that manages reindeer herding work in its own area, social structures among reindeer-herding Sámi in the Nordic countries will be severely affected by climate change. Though many Sámi do not engage in reindeer husbandry themselves, other activities such as farming and fishing also have a strong

12 Kelman, I. and Naess, M., 'Climate change and migration for Scandinavian Sámi: A review of possible impacts', *Climate* 7(4), 2019, p. 47.
13 Hassler, S., Johansson, R., Sjölander, P., Grönberg H. and Damber, L., 'Cause of death in the Sami population of Sweden, 1961–2000', *International Journal of Epidemiology* 34(3), June 2005.

basis in Sámi traditional knowledge. As the Arctic climate shifts, the use of traditional knowledge for future operational decision-making is likely to prove more challenging. While potentially remaining relevant in supporting community structures and coherence, climate change is likely to change the relationship of Sámi to their northern environments and to their traditional livelihoods.[14] These pressures are likely to be exacerbated by national infrastructure developments such as windfarms and hydroelectric dams.

In northern Russia, where the indigenous Nenets people have been hunting and harnessing reindeer during their migrations for centuries, unexpected impacts on health are also occurring. A nomadic people, their unique culture is tied closely to their environment, with reindeer-herding and tundra stewardship playing a crucial role. Temperature changes and shorter winters have led to expanding bodies of water, causing landscape shifts and disrupting traditional migration patterns. Given their isolation in the Russian far north, climate change is already expected to have far-reaching consequences on access to health care, as well as on the social fabric of local indigenous communities reliant upon a threatened species and its grazing lands for their subsistence and cultural life.[15] Women are likely to be at a disadvantage when they require antenatal care, giving an indication of

A Sami woman herding reindeer in Árdni, Norway. Panos / *Abbie Trayler-Smith*

14 Rees, W., Stammler, F., Danks, F. and Vitebsky, P., 'Vulnerability of European reindeer husbandry to global change', *Climate* 87, 2008, pp. 199–217.
15 Amstislavski, P., Zubov, L., Chen, H., Ceccato, P., Pekel, J. and Weedon, J., 'Effects of increase in temperature and open water on transmigration and access to health care by the Nenets reindeer herders in northern Russia', *International Journal of Circumpolar Health* 72, 2013.

the extra vulnerabilities faced by more vulnerable segments of the indigenous communities in these regions.

Sometimes changes are too gradual to be clearly attributable to climate change. As news reports continue to state that it is impossible to attribute single extreme weather events to climate change, as the science is so complex, many indigenous communities in the Arctic are also focused on the more immediate dangers to their lands and ways of life. For example, some Inuit representatives view the opening up of the Arctic to oil and gas and shipping companies as another pressing threat. These developments are themselves a result of warming temperatures reshaping the waterways at the top of the world.

Traditional knowledge and the threat of cultural extinction

There is already some acknowledgement internationally that indigenous peoples, due to their land-stewardship traditions, can assist in stemming the causes of the crisis and even assess the changes at scales and through recorded baselines that are inaccessible for scientific researchers. However, there is still limited understanding at both a national and global level of the true extent of the challenges that indigenous peoples and minority communities will face in the coming decades – indeed, are already facing – as a result of climate change. This is in part due to the inequitable structures of the international climate governance regime. Only nation-state delegations are participants, with other stakeholders relegated to observer status, and the expense of attending multiple meetings a year can be prohibitive.[16] This leaves little space for minority and indigenous populations to participate in these processes, despite their disproportionate vulnerability to climate change impacts in many cases.

While traditional knowledge is invaluable for documenting and adapting to shifts in weather patterns, in many areas this resource is diminishing and with it the ability of communities to respond to climate change impacts. For example, in Andean Bolivia the indigenous practice of environmental observation rituals to predict weather – for example, a red sunset signifies humidity, a yellow moon indicates rain and so on – is now at risk of being lost, with many younger members of the community lacking what was until recently universal knowledge among this group.[17]

Nevertheless, efforts are being made to ensure that the extensive experience of indigenous peoples is not overlooked and is even brought into effective adaptation strategies. It is vital, though, that this process is conducted equitably, with the free, prior and informed consent of the communities in question and with proper protocols, including those safeguarding intellectual property rights. Given their many experiences of intellectual and cultural expropriation by corporations and governments, indigenous activists have repeatedly highlighted that climate change strategies should not simply 'take' traditional knowledge but fully integrate a broader framework of indigenous rights into any adaptation framework.

16   Belfer, E., Ford, J., Maillet, M., Araos, M. and Flynn, M., 'Pursuing an indigenous platform: Exploring ppportunities and constraints for indigenous participation in the UNFCCC', *Global Environmental Politics* 19(1), February 2019, pp. 12–33.

17   De la Riva, M.V., Lindner, A. and Pretzsch, J., 'Assessing adaptation – Climate change and indigenous livelihood in the Andes of Bolivia', *Journal of Agriculture and Rural Development in the Tropics and Subtropics (JARTS)* 114(2), 2013, pp. 109–22.

Rising sea levels in the Pacific: Indigenous communities struggle to keep their homes

The total disappearance of human settlements and their associated ancestral cultures is a problem well understood by those inhabiting the lowest-lying Pacific Islands, comprising nations such as Kiribati, Tuvalu and Vanuatu. Parts of these islands have been all but submerged and a number made partially or fully uninhabitable.

With worst-case 'business as usual' scenarios foreseeing that sea levels worldwide could rise by 2 metres (above year 2000 levels) by 2100, nations built on these islands with the lowest elevations will likely have few options but to reclaim land or depart for other islands or countries elsewhere. With this in mind, the government of Kiribati has pre-emptively purchased land on a larger Pacific island, Fiji, to enable the resettlement of their population.

The Pacific region already struggles with a number of complex societal issues related to both a long colonial history and an increasingly globalized present, with concerns about issues such as sovereignty, human rights, health, education, employment, tourism and cultural sustainability attracting considerable attention and debate. These issues have become all the more acute in the face of rising seawaters. Even the larger and more populous Pacific Islands, such as the Marshall Islands and Fiji, are facing challenges protecting water supplies from storm surges and 'king tides' that not only exacerbate sea-level rises but accelerate the salinization of fresh-water supplies.

Land is crucial to Pacific Islanders' indigenous worldviews and identities. For example, the Fijian concept of *vanua* ties the spiritual identity of a community to its place, making the two inseparable. This is one reason why, despite the considerable challenges of remaining in some areas, Pacific governments such as Fiji and Tuvalu are working with communities to ensure the option of remaining in situ, with a view to maintaining human rights and dignity.[18] At the same time, Kiribati's Migration with Dignity Policy is also working to strengthen international links to the i-Kiribati diaspora with schemes for managing voluntary, temporary labour migration – an approach that could help prevent more permanent forms of migration.

Nevertheless, these choices are stark: loss of land appears inevitable, and some form of adaptation or migration will become necessary. However, the widespread 'normalization' of the idea that climate change may cause the complete loss of many atoll countries is problematic, and also assumes little or limited agency among atoll peoples. Research from Fiji has found that this situation is particularly difficult for the island's youth, who will not only bear the burden of climate change's direct impacts, but will also ultimately shoulder much of the responsibility for ensuring that effective adaptation activities are implemented. This poses particular challenges in a context where decision-making structures remain hierarchical and knowledge on climate change is still limited.[19]

18 Farbotko, C., 'No retreat: Climate change and voluntary immobility in the Pacific Islands', *Migration Policy*, 13 June 2018.

19 Barnett, J., 'The dilemmas of normalising losses from climate change: Towards hope for Pacific atoll countries', *Asia Pacific Viewpoint* 58(1), 2017, pp. 3–13.

A child plays in the rushing sea water that broke through a makeshift sea wall put in place ahead of the spring tide, Tarawa, Kiribati. Panos / *Jocelyn Carlin*

With rising sea levels, it is estimated that millions of indigenous Pacific Islanders will be forced to migrate and resettle elsewhere by 2050.[20] A future that involves the forced relocation of entire communities raises questions that would need to be answered on both transnational and national levels, including strong negotiations with nearby Australia and New Zealand, with the former already pursuing actively hostile policies towards asylum seekers from Asia and elsewhere. The international community is politically, legally and morally unprepared for these outcomes, with a reluctance from international organizations to even discuss or recognize the term 'environmental refugee', much less embed the concept into existing international legislation on refugee protection.[21]

On Fiji, minority groups include Banabans, Rotumans and those native to other Pacific Islands, who remain marginalized socially and politically in different ways. Banabans were resettled in Fiji in 1945 as a result of British-led phosphate mining from the early 1900s, demonstrating how colonial and globalized trade have had lasting 'socio-environmental' impacts on the atolls. Research into this relocation has been able to provide some indication of the needs

20 Höing, N. and Razzaque, J., 'Unacknowledged and unwanted? "Environmental refugees" in search of legal status', *Journal of Global Ethics* 8(1), April 2012, pp. 19–40, https://doi.org/10.1080/17449626.2011.635691

21 *Ibid.*

and requirements of Pacific Islanders should relocation become inevitable.[22] The dynamic of movement spurred by environmental damage by outside actors is exemplified particularly by the movement of Marshall Islanders away from the Bikini Atoll, a site of US nuclear testing in the mid-twentieth century, towards the Kili and Ejit islands, which are now themselves under threat from rising seawaters. Some projections now suggest that many of these 'resettlement' islands could become uninhabitable in coming decades due to contamination of fresh-water supplies by waves.

While much of this section has highlighted the unique vulnerability of these Pacific island nations, it is important also to emphasize their rich cultural heritage and the role their communities can play in strengthening resilience to environmental shocks. In Vanuatu, for example, traditional building techniques could withstand extreme weather impacts when the island was devastated by Cyclone Pam in March 2015, leaving 75,000 people in need of emergency assistance. The death toll remained relatively low due to the robust design of traditional huts known as 'nakamals'. State delegates from Vanuatu have also participated actively in international climate discussions, including in Paris in 2015 and Morocco in 2016, calling for more funding to safeguard traditional knowledge. In 2017 the government launched an environmental sustainability programme foregrounding the use of their traditional principles in climate change adaptation and disaster resilience schemes.

Land rights and the threat of eviction

What the examples discussed already illustrate is that, until the broader backdrop of discrimination is addressed, minorities and indigenous peoples are likely to remain disproportionately vulnerable to climate change. The importance of rights-based approaches to these and other marginalized communities, particularly with regard to land, is illustrated by the well-documented failures and human rights violations associated with climate and environmental programmes that have led to the displacement of communities from their ancestral territory in the name of conservation. Despite maintaining them for centuries in many cases, in contrast to the practices of illegal loggers, plantation developers and other actors, indigenous peoples are often treated by authorities as potential threats to their forests and lands – a perspective that is used to justify their eviction.

However, through their conservation of biological diversity and management of forests and other natural resources, indigenous peoples have demonstrated their unique ability to use natural resources sustainably to play a crucial role in addressing climate change. Indeed, studies have found that indigenous land tenure rights are the most cost-effective way to protect forests, sequester carbon and ultimately mitigate climate change. In some cases, international climate and land governance schemes have recognized this potential and are drawing on indigenous knowledge to improve land stewardship. Yet, as mentioned earlier, global mitigation schemes such as REDD+ continue to be attacked by critics as a form of 'carbon colonialism'.

---

22 Edwards, J., 'Phosphate mining and the relocation of the Banabans to northern Fiji in 1945: Lessons for climate change-forced displacement', *Journal de La Société des Océanistes*, no. 138–9, December 2014, pp. 121–36.

The implications of climate change for food and land tenure security are also of particular concern to pastoralist and other indigenous communities in Kenya, for example. A series of escalating droughts, including the States of Emergency in 2011 and 2017, have driven communities such as Endorois, who live on the shores of Lake Bogoria in the Rift Valley, and Aweer (Dahalo) traditional hunter-gatherers from Lamu, away from their regions in search of pasture or opportunities to work. When communities are forced to move and encroach on neighbouring lands, violence can result. During the 2017 drought, for instance, pastoralists were killed in Laikipia as they moved towards majority settlements to search for grazing for their animals. This highlighted the serious issues with land inequality in Kenya, rooted in part in the colonial history of the country, as Laikipia is commonly known as an area where expatriates have settled. Local Maasai herders have faced similar pressures to other pastoralists, but had previously been permitted to graze on the estates of Laikipia during crisis periods – an arrangement that had helped to minimize potential conflict.

Resource shortages in East Africa: Displacement and forced migration for forest-dwelling peoples and pastoralists
In Uganda, the situation for minorities and indigenous peoples dealing with successive and worsening drought events is particularly dire. These communities, including pastoralists, are working to secure their rights to recognition from the government, including land, while also contending with the deleterious effects of drought and changing weather patterns on their traditional livelihoods. A prior history of discrimination, including dispossession of land, can leave communities ill equipped to response to climate change impacts.

This is the case for the country's marginalized Batwa, an indigenous people removed from the Bwindi Impenetrable Forest in 1991 by the Ugandan government. The community can no longer depend on forest foodstuffs following the eviction, thereby making them food-insecure. As the forced displacement undermined traditional knowledge retention and transmission years ago, the community took to subsistence agriculture to survive. Poor yields related to the changing climate are expected to increase malnutrition rates, while precarious and restricted access to land and casual labour with neighbouring communities are also compounding their food insecurity. Additionally, warmer and wetter rainy seasons are bringing increased incidences of malaria and diarrhoea, further inhibiting the ability of individuals to work the land. Limited knowledge of the new areas of settlement, compared to a developed understanding of the multiple forms of food available in their ancestral forest, will further jeopardize their food security. Even where climate knowledge is established, weather patterns are rapidly changing and making it more difficult to judge when to plant crops. Researchers and non-governmental groups suggest that more inclusive adaptive mechanisms are necessary to respond to the threats posed by climate change so as to ensure food security for groups like Batwa. [23]

23 Lwasa, S., Ford, J., Berrang-Ford, L., Namanya, D., the Indigenous Health Adaptation to Climate Change Research Team, Buyinza, A. and Nabaasa, B., 'Resilience to climate change in Uganda: Policy implications for two marginalized societies', in L.R. Mason and J. Rigg (eds), *People and Climate Change: Vulnerability, Adaptation, and Social Justice*, Oxford, Oxford University Press, 2019, pp. 156–159.

Migration as a consequence of climate change

Migration patterns are very much influenced by climate change, with crop failures and other pressures driving movement elsewhere – a situation that will pose huge challenges for traditional cultures and livelihoods, as well as threaten enjoyment of rights to housing, work, health care and political participation. However, the global migration framework has to date been focused on migration as a result of conflict, with little protection for migration stemming from natural disasters or economic decline as a result of environmental degradation.

The decision to migrate is typically multi-layered and intersects with other factors such as discrimination, security and the search for opportunities elsewhere.[24] While the connection between climate change and migration is sometimes complex, however, there is evidence to suggest that in some cases its role may not be adequately acknowledged, particularly given the at times divisive framing of migration issues in many media outlets.

Central and North America:
The role of climate in driving
migration to the US
Migration to the US from Central America is increasing, and although violence is often cited as a motive for uprooting from countries such as Guatemala, Honduras and El Salvador, climatic shifts may also have a considerable role to play.

A significant share of all employment in Central America is linked to agriculture, with disruption to farming devastating whole communities and migration serving as a common adaptive strategy. While slowing trade, lower prices and crop disease have all contributed to agricultural decline, climate change is also believed to be affecting the quality and frequency of staple crops such as coffee. Many of those being uprooted are indigenous rural labourers who are left with few other options when their crops fail year after year. Particularly vulnerable are indigenous women of this region, who suffer the added pressures of extremely high rates of sexual and gender-based violence. Migrant women and children in the US and Mexico, many of whom are indigenous, may also be targeted for sexual exploitation.

Climate-induced migration to the US has also created ethnic and linguistic minority groups living in relative poverty and unable to access their rights due to discrimination. Migrant workers in the South, who form ethnic minority communities and many of whom are also members of indigenous communities, are increasingly facing climate impacts in their chosen host regions. For example, during the unprecedented Californian wildfires of late 2018, tens of thousands of migrant farmworkers were still picking fruit in hazardous conditions and polluted air. Many reportedly felt compelled to do so because they needed the income and were unable to challenge their employers due to their limited English.

24   For more discussion of this issue, see Mayrhofer, M., 'Climate change, minorities, indigenous peoples and mobility', in MRG, *Key Trends Report 2019: Focus on Climate*, London, June 2019.

Conclusion: minorities, indigenous peoples and the fight against climate change

The troubling picture that emerges is that minorities and indigenous peoples not only suffer disproportionately from climate change in terms of its impacts but are also less likely to benefit from any adaptation or recovery strategies. In response to these pressures, however, community environmental defenders have played a pivotal role in securing action against climate change on local, national and international levels. However, as environmental defenders are often poor, marginalized and belong to discriminated communities, violence directed at them by more powerful entities is a constant threat. In Brazil, a country that has long topped the tables for the most environmental defenders murdered each year, this trend is only likely to increase given the recent election of President Bolsonaro and his assault on indigenous rights since taking office.

Here and across the world, respect for the rights of indigenous communities to their ancestral lands will in particular play a crucial role in boosting their resilience to climate change, while also bolstering global efforts to mitigate its impact through more sustainable stewardship of natural resources. This requires an emphasis on rights and protections, rather than simply focusing on technological fixes. Looking ahead, environmental engineering on a large scale, including the alarming propositions of planetary-scale geo-engineering to mitigate future climate change, may yet mean that minorities and indigenous peoples will fare even worse. For example, extrapolating from the harm already being caused to indigenous communities from the remodelling of the Amazon River, the largest river in terms of water capacity in the world, can give some indication of the potential dangers of future irreversible geo-engineering projects that are currently being proposed, such as greenhouse gas removal, solar radiation management through ocean re-fertilization, mass planting of high albedo crops or snow forest clearance.

These examples serve as reminders that our planet's ecological systems are intricately connected and global in nature, and that what today has the greatest effect on sometimes remote minority and indigenous communities could one day be felt by us all. The issues being faced by the poorest, the most marginalized and the most discriminated against must become a priority for states and part of the agenda at international climate and biodiversity negotiations. Anthropogenic climate change and irreversible damage to entire ecosystems threaten to disrupt everything. The experiences already being faced by the world's most vulnerable communities should serve as a clear warning to governments, international agencies and businesses everywhere.

CASE STUDY

Tuvalu: 'We have a right to stay in our God-given islands'

Soseala Tinilau, besides serving as the Director of Environment in Tuvalu's Ministry of Foreign Affairs, Trade, Tourism, Environment and Labour, is also President of the Tuvalu Islands Football Association (TIFA). In 2018, as he explains to MRG, the Tuvalu team performed in the Confederation of Independent Football Associations (CONIFA)'s World Cup – an opportunity that was used not only to showcase the country's football skills but also the challenges posed by climate change.

Climate change has impacted on Tuvalu and its inhabitants due to its resource-poor, low-lying, fragile and remote physical nature. These are some of the environmental effects I have noticed:

- Constant seawater inundation, which has caused severe damage to Tuvalu's only staple crop, threatening our food supply.
- Sea level rise, especially during king tides, inundating most low-lying areas of the islands including the airstrip, affecting people's daily travel.
- Increasingly intense cyclones like Tropical Cyclone Pam in 2015, which severely damaged crops, houses, hospitals and livestock. It completely wiped out three uninhabited islets which people depend on for firewood, food and shelter.
- Severe erosion of beachfronts, especially on the western sides of the islands, which triggers quarrels among land owners.
- Severe droughts which brought the country to its knees as most families were without water.
- Decreasing reef resources due to rising sea temperature, contributing to coral bleaching.

My motivation for drawing attention to climate change during our participation in the 2018 CONIFA World Cup is due to the fact that we were representing Tuvalu and because of the issues we faced back home. Even with these uncertainties, we can become resilient if we work together to adapt to the adverse impacts of climate change, and we can use football as a tool for advocacy. As you know, football is the beautiful game, and more people can relate themselves to this.

I made appointments especially with sportswriters and television stations to be interviewed during the games, and that's where I mentioned the plight of our country due to the adverse impacts of climate change and asked the audience to help reduce their emissions, because a small act goes a long way. We have a right to stay in our God-given islands.

I wish to see countries, especially those who are parties to the Paris Agreement, do their fair share and expedite the implementation of the Paris Agreement, increase their National Determined Contributions to reduce emissions and to make the transition to renewable energy.

Indigenous Rights and Resistance to Climate Change: Progress and Setbacks since the Paris Agreement

Nicole Girard

The adoption of the Paris Agreement in December 2015 was a milestone in humanity's collective struggle against a rapidly changing climate. For indigenous peoples, it represented the culmination of their efforts to rightfully participate in global climate discussions. It was the first climate change treaty to directly acknowledge the rights of indigenous peoples, and it was also pioneering in its inclusion of indigenous representatives throughout the negotiation process.

Despite this, however, troubling gaps remain. References to indigenous rights are only in the preamble and are not legally binding – mention of their rights in the body of the agreement had been included in early drafts but was subsequently removed – while the only other mention of indigenous peoples is in the section addressing adaptation, specifically recognizing how traditional knowledge systems are important for potential climate change adaptation solutions.

The Paris Agreement was the result of two decades of climate talks within the United Nations Framework Convention on Climate Change (UNFCCC). Despite very little engagement with indigenous peoples both leading up to the UNFCCC and in its periodic assessment reports, indigenous peoples have long been sounding the alarm on climate change. Arctic peoples, Sámi in particular, were among the first to report that the climate was changing and it was having an impact on their livelihoods.

As stewards of fragile ecosystems, with highly detailed knowledge of how to exist and adapt to these often difficult terrains developed over centuries, they and other indigenous peoples are collectively asserting their right to set the terms of the climate change debate. But why until now have indigenous peoples been given so little space in international climate change and adaptation discussions?

Exposure, Sensitivity and Adaptive Capacity

'We, the indigenous peoples of the world, are more exposed and vulnerable to the negative effects and consequences [of climate change] for which indigenous peoples pay a high price, even if we are not responsible for this situation.'
– Rose Cunningham Kain, Miskitu indigenous leader, Nicaragua [1]

Changes in the climate are disproportionately impacting indigenous peoples. While the fragility of many indigenous environments has often been highlighted as a key cause of this disproportionate impact, this alone does not properly capture the role that historic marginalization and discrimination has also played, nor the remarkable resilience that has enabled indigenous peoples to survive and maintain their cultural identities in their traditional territories.

It is more constructive, then, to consider the established framework of vulnerability as exposure to the effects of climate change, sensitivity to its impact and adaptability in the face of these changes. Indigenous peoples are not only especially exposed to climate change due to the location of many communities in territories with glaciers, lakes, forests, grasslands, coastlines and other ecosystems that are especially threatened by climate change, but are also more sensitive to its effects as a result of their strong attachment to their ancestral lands. This is why, when indigenous communities are forced by natural disasters or other shocks to leave their territories and their resources, they not only face the loss of traditional livelihoods but also the severing of deep cultural and spiritual ties. Their ability to respond, on the other hand, is often constrained by the broader context of discrimination they face from state authorities and the majority population – in particular, lack of recognition of their rights to land and natural resources. This situation has also enabled the encroachment of dams, mines and plantations on their lands, with conservation and climate mitigation projects now also posing an increasing threat.

Ethiopia's Nyangatom

'The external perception is that pastoralists are very vulnerable to climate instability. It is true that droughts are highly stressful and traumatic, and that climate-sensitive diseases are increasing, but pastoralism in Africa was born from a context of poor soils, which encouraged the sustainable use of natural resources and population mobility. The knowledge and adaptability that pastoralists have acquired are great assets in the current context of instability. Farmers are more likely than herders to starve in a drought.'
– Paul Kanyinke Sena, in a 2013 report [2] written as a member of the UN Permanent Forum on Indigenous Issues

1   Kain, R., 'The grandmothers of the Wangki' in Tebtebba, *Indigenous Women, Climate Change & Forests 9*, 2011.
2   UN Economic and Social Council, 'Study on resilience, traditional knowledge and capacity building for pastoralist communities in Africa', Permanent Forum on Indigenous Issues, 12th session, 2013.

These intersecting pressures and their impact on indigenous peoples are illustrated by the experiences of the semi-nomadic agro-pastoralist Nyangatom community in Ethiopia. With traditional territories encompassing the southern lowlands, including the Omo and Mago national parks, their livestock is central to their food security, culture and self-identity, as is their cultivation of sorghum and its associated rituals. Their elders recall changes to rain patterns starting in 1989, which became more severe after 1998, with a gradual decline in precipitation leading to protracted drought in 2011, four to five years after failed rains. The UN declared a famine the same year, but by this time much of the Nyangtom livestock had already died.[3] They have since largely abandoned sorghum farming and the Kubish river, once a central cultural meeting point, has now dried up, in part due to the spread of an invasive evergreen shrub (*prosopis juliflora*) that has been blamed for sucking water from the landscape and affecting grassland availability.[4]

Nyangatom have suffered a range of impacts as a result of climate change and its associated social impacts, including widespread food insecurity and the disruption of traditional sharing practices, that have left many reliant on aid. Women are especially affected and are more dependent now on their husbands. The upsetting of traditional seasonal calendars and their associated time marking rituals, which lies at the heart of the Nyangatom's cultural identity, have resulted in an existential shock to the community. They remain unsure of when to hold these ceremonies and are reportedly considering changing the names of the months in order to attempt to rebalance the calendar.

The challenges Nyangatom face are compounded by their social exclusion. Pastoralist communities in Ethiopia have long contended with climate extremes, and their adaptive techniques have traditionally included the ability to roam to better pastures for their livestock during periods of environmental stress. However, land encroachment and fragmentation of their mobility routes by the development of large-scale sugar plantations and national parks, where grazing is prohibited, means this solution is no longer possible. Due to enduring discrimination by the government of Ethiopia, land rights that are enshrined in the Constitution for pastoralist communities are circumvented by the authorities.

Notwithstanding these challenges, including discriminatory barriers that prevent them from implementing many tried and tested responses to drought and other environmental strains, Nyangtom continue to engage their survival strategies in the face of adversity. Among other measures, they have moved away from rain-fed agriculture to flood-fed agriculture along the banks of the Omo River, with maize and beans prioritized as they have a shorter maturing period than sorghum. Cattle are also led to pastures further away in mountain areas and remain there for extended periods of time. These examples illustrate how community members have been able to cope with a changing environment by adapting their traditional knowledge to new contexts.[5]

---

3   Troeger, S., '"Everything that is happening now is beyond our capacity": Nyangatom livelihoods under threat', in D.Nakashima, *Indigenous Knowledge for Climate Change Adaptation and Assessment*, Cambridge University Press, 2018.

4   Mehari, Z., 'The invasion of *Prosopis juliflora* and Afar pastoral livelihoods in the Middle Awash area of Ethiopia', *Ecological Processes* 4(1), October 2015.

5   Troeger, *op. cit.*

A portrait of an elderly Nyangatom man in Omo Valley, Ethiopia.

Alamy

Traditional knowledge

'Indigenous knowledge is a systematic way of knowing. It holds its own methodologies and validation processes, and it cannot be and should not be validated by science. It's a living process that continues to build upon the knowledge acquired today as well as from the past and will manifest itself in different ways into the future.'
– Dalee Sambo Dorough, Chair, Inuit Circumpolar Council[6]

Traditional knowledge and its use for climate change monitoring, mitigation and adaptation is increasingly becoming a focus of both the scientific community and broader global climate change discussions. The Intergovernmental Panel on Climate Change (IPCC), a UN body tasked with producing periodic assessment reports under the UNFCCC, did not mention indigenous knowledge in their reports from the 1990s, but references steadily increase to over 400 mentions of indigenous peoples or indigenous knowledge in the most recent report, in 2014.[7]

There have been some enduring misunderstandings about the nature

6   Presentation at Arctic Frontiers conference, Norway, January 2019.
7   Nakashima, D., Rubis, J. and Krupnik, I., 'Indigenous knowledge for climate change assessment and adaptation: Introduction', in D. Nakashima (ed.), *Indigenous Knowledge for Climate Change Assessment and Adaptation*, Cambridge University, 2018.

of indigenous traditional knowledge, often stemming from biases within Western science about the nature of these knowledge systems. Indigenous traditional knowledge is adaptive, fluid and diverse. It exists within local socio-cultural systems, largely collectively owned and shared, and is part of a larger holistic worldview and its related set of practices. It is flexible in how it incorporates new learnings on the basis of trial and error, integrating new experiences, and focusing on qualitative findings. It is passed on orally and is primarily concerned with daily livelihoods, survival and cultural continuity.[8] Knowledge is often gendered as well, with men and women holding different yet complementary sets of knowledge and related practices.

The neglect of indigenous knowledge is in part the result of limited awareness of local conditions. The scientific community stems from misunderstandings around indigenous knowledge itself. In one now well-known case, indigenous Andean farmers established their annual planting calendars based on the visibility of the Pleiades star cluster, forecasting the amount and quality of rainfall in the next growing season. Scientists were sceptical about this method. How could they accurately predict precipitation based on stars that are light years away? After interdisciplinary collaboration between an anthropologist, meteorologist and a climatologist, they 'discovered' that the visibility of the star cluster was an indicator of humidity levels in the upper atmosphere, which was an accurate predictor of the El Niño, when rains are less reliable.[9]

Whereas climate change science is often more focused at the global level – for example, through tonnes of carbon in the atmosphere and global mean temperatures – indigenous climate change knowledge is much more focused on changes at the local level.[10] Climate scientists are still building their understanding of local climate changes, often based on the observations of indigenous peoples. In a case from Mongolia, pastoralist herders had reported changes in the type of rain they had been receiving, from soft rain that penetrated the soil to hard rain that just ran off, as well as patchy rain that did not fully regenerate whole pasture areas. Yet standard meteorological measurements of rain, measuring only the volume of rain rather than its quality, would not have recorded any significant changes since the mean amount of rain had not changed substantively.

It is these very specific, empirical understandings of their ecosystem that demonstrate the value of indigenous perspectives when assessing and modelling climate impacts at a local level. There is a concern, however, that as the value of traditional knowledge and its insights for climate change monitoring and mitigation increase, it will be isolated from the larger indigenous rights framework. This brings broader questions of power and participation into play. As noted previously, indigenous rights are not a legally binding component of the Paris Agreement, and indigenous peoples have a long history of being sidelined in climate discussions – a situation that still prevails today. Analysis of the level of involvement of indigenous peoples at international climate

8   Conservation of Arctic Flora and Fauna (CAFF), *Arctic Traditional Knowledge and Wisdom: Changes in the North American Arctic*, CAFF Assessment Series Report No. 14, April 2017, p. 12.

9   Nakashima, Rubis and Krupnik, *op. cit.*

10   Foyer, J. and Kervran, D., 'Objectifying traditional knowledge, re-enchanting the struggle against climate change', in A. Stefan, J. Foyer, E. Morena (eds.), *Globalising the Climate: COP21 and the Climatisation of Global Debates*, Routledge, 2017.

negotiations, for example, suggests that their participation at forums such as the UNFCCC Conference of the Parties (COP) is still largely confined to side events and observer status rather than substantive decision-making.[11]

This situation cannot be transformed solely by extracting indigenous knowledge for the benefit of mainstream climate response structures. Rather, the value of this resource needs to be respectfully integrated alongside a wider rights-based framework for indigenous peoples – spanning territorial ownership, self-determination, consultation and participation – that promotes their roles as equal partners in the process.

Rights and resistance

'When I was a kid, in the community, we used to stay in the forest for a month, in the summertime. We found out that some people, invaders, had come to our land, taking our land. Because at that time we didn't have any land titles [but] after some fight, we had our land titles. But that was in the eighties, and if you see now, that land, taken by other people, are all cleared, no forest there. The rest, my community and the indigenous community, that we protected with the land titles, we have forests, and we have biodiversity. We still have all the resources there because we depend on that. So that means that we need

to continue in the effort to provide or help titling the lands of indigenous peoples. That is a clear message.'
– Johnson Cerda, an Ecuadorian Quechua activist[12]

At the centre of the intersection of indigenous rights and climate change is land, territorial governance and communal ownership. Environmental groups have repeatedly highlighted how strengthening land and resource rights for indigenous peoples is an 'undervalued approach to mitigating climate change'.[13] One study has estimated that at least 24 per cent of all carbon stored above ground in rainforests was being managed by indigenous and local communities – amounting to some 54,546 million metric tonnes of carbon (MtC), some 250 times the volume attributable to worldwide air travel in 2015 – while around a tenth of all the carbon stored in tropical forests was located in collective forestlands without formal recognition, placing them at risk of logging and clearance.[14] Indeed, legal recognition and enforcement of community land rights has been shown to lower carbon emissions and deforestation: a recent comparative study of deforestation levels in indigenous and non-indigenous areas found that 'deforestation of indigenous community forests in Brazil would likely have been 22 times higher without their legal recognition.'[15]

11 Comberti, C., Thornton, T. and Korodimou, M., 'Addressing indigenous peoples' marginalisation at international climate negotiations: Adaptation and resilience at the margins', Working Paper, Environmental Change Institute (ECI), University of Oxford, 2016.
12 2018 United Nations Climate Change Conference, 'CI: LCIP Platform: a force for transformative change in raising ambition from natural climate solutions', Side event, 7 December 2018, Kotowice, Poland.
13 World Resources Institute and Rights + Resources, *Securing Rights, Combating Climate Change: How Strengthening Community Forests Rights Mitigates Climate Change*, 2014, p. 7.
14 Rights +Resources et al., *Towards a Global Baseline of Carbon Storage in Collective Lands: An Updated Analysis of Indigenous Peoples' and Local Communities' Contributions to Climate Change Mitigation*, November 2016.
15 World Resources Initiative and Rights + Resources, op. cit., p. 3.

This intersection of communal land rights and the global struggle to mitigate climate change, as well as the disproportionate exposure of indigenous peoples themselves to its impacts, explains the prominent role indigenous activists are now playing in protest movements against climate inaction all over the world. This has been particularly evident in Brazil, where indigenous communities have for decades resisted the encroachment of governments, corporations and loggers on their land: their protests have taken on an added urgency since the recent election of President Jair Bolsonaro, who swept to power on a platform that included, among other measures, a commitment to dismantling indigenous land rights protections in favour of logging, mining and other interests. In January 2019, on his first day in office, he transferred indigenous land demarcation responsibilities to the pro-agrobusiness agriculture ministry. According to indigenous non-governmental organization (NGO) Imazon, illegal land seizures had resulted in a loss of 12 square kilometres of forest in indigenous territories over the first three months of 2019 – double the area taken over the same period the previous year.[16]

These measures have been met with a strong response from indigenous communities who, building on their long history of protest, have quickly mobilized against the planned rollback of their rights. Between 24 and 26 April 2019, for instance, over 4,000 indigenous people travelled thousands of kilometres for their annual Free Land Camp action in the capital, Brasilia. While it has served as a key indigenous resistance gathering throughout its 15 years of existence, the Free Land Camp was particularly meaningful this year as Bolsonaro's anti-indigenous rights rhetoric has already emboldened those who wish to see the Amazon opened up for business. The three-day protest included marches, speeches at the Senate and a vigil in front of the Supreme Federal Court. A statement by Articulação dos Povos Indígenas do Brasil, an indigenous umbrella organization, condemned the Bolsonaro administration as 'anti-national, predatory, ethnocidal, genocidal and ecocidal', and concluded with the promise: 'We will resist, no matter what!'[17]

The Salween Peace Park, Karen State, Myanmar

Unfortunately, the tactics of the Bolsonaro administration are familiar to governments around the world, whereby indigenous environmental stewardship is generally ignored or overlooked, and a top-down conservationist approach to forest management and climate mitigation takes priority. And yet in situations in which governments do not recognize indigenous land rights, indigenous communities are still asserting their customary rights to forest stewardship and their right to be at the forefront of climate change mitigation and adaptation strategies.

The Salween Peace Park, established in December 2018 in Mutraw District, Karen State, Myanmar, was the indigenous Karen response to the Myanmar government's disregard of indigenous rights and climate change

16 Amnesty International, 'Brazil: Risk of bloodshed in the Amazon unless government protects Indigenous peoples from illegal land seizures and logging', 7 May 2019.

17 https://www.facebook.com/notes/apib-articula%C3%A7%C3%A3o-dos-povos-ind%C3%ADgenas-do-brasil/we-have-been-resisting-for-519-years-and-we-will-continue-to-resist/2277136669223156/

mitigation, despite the impacts it is already having on the Karen people. Spanning almost 5,500 square kilometres and more than 340 villages, it is the combined effort of local Karen communities, Karen civil society organizations (CSOs) and Karen National Union district leaders. The Peace Park was established through a series of public consultations, beginning in 2016, and the drafting of the Salween Peace Park (SPP) Charter by a 47-member steering committee and its subsequent approval through a referendum that was endorsed by 75.1 per cent of the population.

Paul Sein Twa, Executive Director of KESAN, a Karen CSO leading the establishment of the park, explains:

'There are three pillars of the SPP Charter. One is peace and self-determination, meaning we can manage ourselves and live free from militarization. The second is environmental integrity, whereby we will protect the river, for example, and provide the wildlife sanctuaries and maintain forest corridors for protection of key species such as tigers. The third pillar is cultural survival, whereby our traditional land tenure and cultural heritage is preserved and revitalized.[18]

As the Karen are experiencing negative impacts of climate change, the Charter specifically notes how the people of the SPP must prioritize the implementation of climate change mitigation strategies, including crop diversification, water management, avoidance of deforestation and soil degradation. The government of Myanmar, however, has not recognized the establishment of the park, and threats to the environmental integrity of the park remain, including a proposed dam on the Salween River, the Hatgyi dam.

In contrast to the Salween Peace Park is the Reef to Ridge Project, a US$21 million conservation initiative that encompasses 800,000 acres of the south-eastern Tanintharyi region, Myanmar, also in the traditional territory of the Karen. The project is implemented under the UN Development Programme (UNDP) and financed by the Global Environmental Facility (GEF) and the UK-based charity Flora and Fauna International (FFI). The project has been accused of not respecting the rights of the Karen. In a formal complaint to the GEF, the Conservation Alliance Tanawthari (CAT), of which KESAN is a member, stated that no processes to secure free, prior and informed consent (FPIC) had been undertaken and that there was little knowledge or awareness of the project among local residents. 'A vast majority of communities throughout proposed project areas,' it reported, 'have never even been informed of the existence of the project.'[19] Project Manager Mark Grindley, who supervises FFI's conservation programme in Tanintharyi, was paraphrased in a *Guardian* newspaper article as saying, 'Consulting every village before the start of the project would have been impractical ... The plan was to get consent as needed over the project's duration.'[20]

For critics of the project – described by Paul Sein Twa as 'an example of top-down, government and UN conservation programmes that don't do proper consultations' – it is an important reminder of the pitfalls of implementing environmental programmes without

---

18 Interview with author, 21 March 2019, Thailand.
19 Conservation Alliance Tanawthari (CAT), 'Complaint letter to the Global Environment Facility concerning the Ridge to Reef Project and the violation of the rights of indigenous people', 16 July 2018.
20 Joshua Carroll, 'Displaced villagers in Myanmar at odds with UK charity over land conservation', *Guardian*, 2 November 2018.

respecting the needs and perspectives of the communities affected. 'They often don't recognize local and indigenous communities' customary rights to their resources and lands,' he continues. 'They very much rely on technology and collecting data to monitor the environment, in order to expand protected areas.' The danger is that, while community-led conservation projects could deliver significant benefits to both the environment and local residents, imposing these programmes without meaningful consultation ultimately replicates the marginalization of indigenous peoples in the region: 'It takes away indigenous Karen's rights to manage land and territories.'

Reframing the discussion

The concept of 'environmental conservation' is largely at odds with indigenous worldviews, as it makes a separation between humans and the rest of the ecosystem: many indigenous peoples see themselves as stewards tasked with protecting their ecosystems, with customary land use practices specifically designed to support this. As discussed earlier, removing stewardship over their territories often only contributes to the destruction of these lands and forests, resulting in the massive release of carbon and the acceleration of climate change.

Unfortunately, in many countries where indigenous rights are weak or unacknowledged, 'conservation' can often be a top-down process driven by the belief that governments are best positioned to manage natural ecosystems and to determine, establish and manage national conservation

agendas. This results in what has been dubbed 'fortress conservation,' where indigenous peoples are locked out from access to their lands, which in turn can result in forced evictions, violence and even killings of indigenous peoples.[21]

Despite the increase in protected conservation areas since the 1970s, some governments are getting the message that holistic ecosystem stewardship offers an effective alternative to the top-down model – an approach that goes hand in hand with indigenous rights to land. This is reflected in *Buen Vivir*, a concept that prioritizes a holistic view of living ecosystems where humans are only one part of a larger whole. It is the Spanish translation of *Sumak Kawsay*, a concept of 'the good life' as understood by the Quechua and other peoples of the Andes, described as a way of existing that is 'community-centric, ecologically-balanced and culturally-sensitive'.[22] The concept, advanced by indigenous activism, has been enshrined in the Constitutions of Ecuador and Bolivia. It represents a rejoinder to the dominant capitalist, neo-liberal, anthropocentric worldview where nature is exploited for short-term gain.[23]

Buen Vivir has also made its way into indigenous-led approaches to climate change. The Indigenous Peoples' Biocultural Climate Change Assessment Initiative (IPCCA) was established as a research initiative that aims to support the development of indigenous-led adaptation strategies and integrate indigenous voices into policy discussions. The IPCCA works with indigenous communities to develop and apply their own frameworks for

21 Tauli-Corpuz, V., Alcorn, J. and Molnar, A., *Cornered by Protected Areas, Rights + Resources Initiative*, June 2018.
22 Salazar, J.F., 'Buen Vivir: South America's rethinking of the future we want', The Conservation, 24 July 2015.
23 Gudynas, E., 'Buen Vivir: Today's tomorrow', *Development* 54(4), 2011.

assessing climate change impacts in their territories, through collaboration with Western science. Building and strengthening *Buen Vivir* is central to the IPCCA's vision. The IPCCA offers a unique approach to climate change assessments, with its focus on indigenous-led monitoring of localized impacts of climate change, and takes a holistic approach to climate change phenomena. For this reason, the IPCAA uses the term 'indigenous biocultural system' to describe these complex relationships between indigenous peoples, their territories and their rights to these territories.

Systems synergies

IPCAA is just one example of a growing number of collaborations between indigenous peoples and Western science, and the building of synergies between different approaches to climate change monitoring, adaptation and mitigation. The Arctic region has also been leading the way in participatory approaches to tackling climate change. The Arctic Council, established in 1997, is an intergovernmental forum comprising eight Arctic states as members and six organizations representing Arctic Indigenous peoples as permanent participants. Though the participating organizations still face some barriers, such as financial constraints, the existence of the Arctic Council is nevertheless significant as indigenous organizations discuss directly with state representatives on issues relating to Arctic governance and climate change.[24] In 2005, under the guidance of the Arctic Council, the *Arctic Climate Impact Assessment* was released. The report was innovative not only in its scope and evaluation of Arctic climate

change, but also in its participation of indigenous peoples and incorporation of traditional knowledge. It was one of the first scientific reports that used the observations of indigenous peoples to support and build on scientific findings, which sought to validate the experiences of indigenous peoples and provide a more holistic understanding of Arctic climate change.[25]

These participatory approaches were further extended to community-based climate change monitoring networks under the Bering Sea Sub-Network (BSSN) implemented by the Aleut International Association from 2009 to 2014. The BSSN project utilized a regional indigenous observation network across Bering Sea states to work in collaboration with scientists at the University of Alaska and the Alaska Native Science Commission to produce data that was both 'scientifically defensible' and based on traditional knowledge. Research assistants from the community were trained to collect quantitative and qualitative observations from local knowledge holders that could then be used to guide policy making and resource protection.[26] This is just one example of how knowledge co-production can facilitate participation of indigenous peoples in climate change monitoring and adaptation.

Local Communities and Indigenous Peoples Platform

At the global level, progress is being made towards the full participation of indigenous peoples in climate change discussions. In particular, the Local Communities and Indigenous Peoples Platform (LCIPP) was established at the 21st session of the Conference of

24 International Polar Year (IPY), *Understanding Earth's Polar Challenges: International Polar Year 2007-2008*, WMO and ICSU, 2011, p. 577.
25 *Ibid.*
26 CAFF, Project Summary: Being Sea Sub-Network II, 2015.

the Parties (COP21) to the UNFCCC in Paris 2015 to strengthen local and indigenous responses to climate change. After consultation with indigenous representatives and civil society groups regarding the purpose, structure and content of the Platform, the LCIPP's Facilitative Working Group was officially operationalized at the COP24 in December 2018. The working group will include seven indigenous representatives, hailing from different socio-cultural regions of the world, alongside seven government representatives. It has a mandate to foster dialogue with bodies and processes both under and outside of the UNFCCC.

The purpose of the LCIPP is threefold: to strengthen the knowledge and practices of local communities and indigenous peoples to address climate change; to facilitate the exchange of experience and sharing of best practices on mitigation and adaptation, and to enhance the engagement of local communities and indigenous peoples in the UNFCCC process. The Platform aims to strengthen and protect traditional knowledge systems in the response to climate change, in line with indigenous peoples' right to FPIC as the holders of this knowledge, with the ultimate aim of integrating diverse knowledge systems into national and international action on climate change.

The establishment of the LCIPP has been hailed as a significant milestone in the recognition of the key role indigenous peoples can play in the collective global action against climate change. But this engagement needs to keep growing. In the words of Michael Charles, a Navajo (Dine) youth activist: 'We will now embark on a process

to breathe life into the Platform using our resilience, knowledge, and rights with equal representation between states and indigenous peoples. However, our millennia of experience in ecological guardianship should not be restricted to one Platform.'[27]

Moving forward

'It's true that the indigenous voices are not heard by decision-makers. And that can be fixed, by making us the decision-makers. More self-determination will make it easier for us to adapt to climate change.'
– Aili Keskitalo, President of the Sámi Parliament of Norway[28]

The Paris Agreement binds each of its 196 signatories to prepare, communicate and maintain successive nationally determined contributions (NDCs), their post-2020 climate actions to reduce emissions and adapt to climate change. As of April 2019, 186 parties have submitted their NDCs. The importance of indigenous knowledge, as discussed in this chapter, is recognized in this text: signatories are obliged to develop their NDCs 'guided by the best available science and, as appropriate, traditional knowledge, knowledge of indigenous peoples and local knowledge systems' (Article 7.5 of the Paris Agreement).

Despite this progress, there are indications that it may take time for governments – many of whom still do not recognize their indigenous communities as such and/or engage in discriminatory practices against them – to meaningfully implement these commitments. In the case of Africa, while 44 of the 54 signatories had submitted their NDCs as of

---

27 Closing Plenary Statement at 2018 United Nations Climate Change Conference, Katowice, Poland, December 2018.

28 Arctic Frontiers 2019 (end of first session), Norway, 21 January 2019.

January 2019, only nine of these made references to indigenous or traditional knowledge.[29] In order for states to collectively reach their Paris Agreement goals, more attention must be paid to the crucial role indigenous peoples can play in climate mitigation and adaptation.

Indigenous knowledge is just one such facet of this participation. Climate change is already having a disproportionate impact on indigenous peoples. These effects, however, are intertwined with the added burden of policies and practices that deny them the rights enshrined in the UN Declaration on the Rights of Indigenous Peoples (UNDRIP), such as the right to self-determination and rights over their lands, territories and resources.

All responses to climate change must prioritize a human rights based approach, in line with international and regional human rights instruments, while understanding that the effects of climate change and their mitigation will affect marginalized groups differently, including women and minority populations. Finally, solutions to reduce the impact of climate change need to be designed in close and meaningful consultation with indigenous communities, aiming to directly assist local adaptation goals, create genuine partnerships and promote collaborations that integrate indigenous perspectives and ways of knowing into climate adaptation strategies.

---

29 Sena, K., 'Traditional knowledge key in achieving Africa's climate goals', IUCN, 22 January 2019.

CASE STUDY

Canada: 'Everything is interconnected – if you remove one element the others topple over'

Ashley Daniel, a Dakota Ojibway indigenous youth environmental activist and UN Youth Delegate, tells Alicia Kroemer about how her upbringing by the lake and forests of Swan Lake First Nation has informed her life and work since.

I grew up on the reserve surrounded by nature, living in harmony with it in a sustainable lifestyle. I first got interested in climate change when I was 10 years old and watched my neighbour gathering rain water and composting on the reserve. I was really interested and curious to see what they were doing and why. I'm also interested in how technology in harmony with nature could potentially help our environment and our people. When I think about the environment, I think about who we are as indigenous people. I think about the violence done to the land and people through colonialism, through resource extraction.

Water, air, land, all of it, the sun, moon, ocean, they are all sacred and connected. As we see it in indigenous culture, everything is interconnected – if you remove one element the others topple over. Life is circular and holistic. We eat the plants that grow from the Earth and breathe the air around us. Industries pollute water, the Earth and the air – all of these elements we need to live. But people around the world are now opening up their eyes and seeing this in the way that we see it. But it is not just opening up our eyes but also taking action – the Earth requires urgent action as how we are going right now, it is a downward spiral.

The Earth is our mother: we come from her, we are part of her. This was something I knew growing up surrounded by nature. You cannot just take and take and take from the Earth, you must also give back. We have to replant trees; we have to honour her water. Our mother is dying because of climate change. It is not just humanity that is affected, it is our animal, insect and bird relatives who are also dying. They don't have a voice to communicate to us that they are being hurt, that their homes are being destroyed because of us. It is a very selfish thing to not think about all the living creatures who also live on this planet who are negatively impacted by environmental destruction. They deserve to be here just as much as we do.

A portrait of Ashley Daniel, a Dakota Ojibway indigenous youth environmental activist. Photo supplied by Alicia Kroemer.

Because the youth are not afraid to say how it is, they are not bound to anything – we just care about the future of the planet which we are growing up in. We are more impacted than our parents and grandparents by climate change. We see a problem and we want to change it. If we can come together collectively, regardless of where you are from and take action, we can be effective. The word is out, the ones that are advocating are becoming stronger and stronger.

There are a lot of aims to discuss in dismantling old power systems in Canada for indigenous issues. We need recommendations to the plastics and beef industries. Our Earth cannot do anything with the plastics we pollute it with: it is not giving back, it is only doing harm. That is a major issue I will be advocating for at the UN.

My ancestors moved around the land and took only things that they could travel with. They did not leave waste. In indigenous culture you leave the land as you found it. My ancestors would have words that I cannot translate in English to express the sorrow they feel about the present state of the world.

Indigenous peoples are first-line defenders against state and extractive industries because we are not afraid to say no. We also have the United Nations Declaration on the Rights of Indigenous Peoples (UNDRIP) as a protective document that we can stand on to hold these states and industries accountable, not only to indigenous peoples, but to all people to protect the environment which provides life for us all. We need more people in the government system saying no with us too.

Climate Change, Minorities, Indigenous Peoples and Mobility

Monika Mayrhofer

'The human rights risks posed by human mobility can be particularly severe for those disproportionately affected by climate change. For example, the displacement of indigenous peoples and the potential loss of their traditional lands, territories and resources threaten their cultural survival, traditional livelihoods and right to self-determination.'[*]

Introduction

The interconnections between climate change and mobility have attracted increasing public, political and academic attention in recent years. At first glance, the relationship between climate change and migration seems quite clear-cut and obvious: climate change is associated with a wide range of harmful phenomena such as more intensive and frequent rainfall, heatwaves, droughts, floods, cyclones or rising sea levels. It follows, then, that an increase in extreme weather events or other climate change-related threats will endanger homes, communities, infrastructures and livelihoods, making it increasingly difficult for people to live in places particularly exposed to these impacts.

However, taking a closer look, it becomes clear that exposure to natural hazards is only one aspect with regard to the consequences of these events in general and in particular to the decision to migrate. Climate change interacts with many other factors, such as wealth, population density, economic and political structures, disaster response systems and different forms of inequalities,

---

[*]   UNHRC, 'Addressing human rights protection gaps in the context of migration and displacement of persons across international borders resulting from the adverse effects of climate change and supporting the adaptation and mitigation plans of developing countries to bridge the protection gaps', A/HRC/38/21, para. 19, 23 April 2018.

marginalization and discrimination. The Intergovernmental Panel on Climate Change (IPCC) has pointed out that 'risks are unevenly distributed and are generally greater for disadvantaged people and communities in countries at all levels of development.'[1]

This is equally true for climate change-related migration. The interrelation between climate change and mobility is a multi-causal and complex phenomenon, where different forms and structures of inequality and marginalization play a decisive role. In general, climate change is associated with a broad variety of different migration responses, such as displacement, labour migration, evacuations, relocations, eviction, circular migration, permanent and short-term migration. Moreover, migration in the context of climate change may not only be understood as a last resort in response to natural disasters or other weather extremes, but also as a means to adjust successfully to the reality of a changing environment – migration as adaptation, in effect. Furthermore, instead of pushing migration, climate change can also prevent or interrupt mobility: for example, nomadic communities might be faced with a disruption of their traditional migratory routes due to a deteriorating environment.

Minorities and indigenous communities are specifically affected by climate change. The United Nations Human Rights Council (UNHRC) has repeatedly voiced its concern that 'adverse effects of climate change are felt most acutely by those segments of the population that are already in vulnerable situations owing to factors such as geography,

poverty, gender, age, indigenous or minority status, national or social origin, birth or other status and disability.'[2] UN human rights bodies have furthermore pointed out that climate change has had and will have a particular adverse effect on 'already marginalized groups including children, older persons, persons with disabilities, women at risk, migrant workers, indigenous peoples, minorities and the poor', with impacts that may increase the risk of forced migration.[3] However, conceptualizing minority members and indigenous communities merely as 'victims' of climate change-related impacts falls short of the crucial role they are able to play in mitigating and adapting to climate change, including climate change-related mobility. Indigenous peoples in particular are now recognized as agents of adaptation and mitigation, with well-established knowledge systems and practices that are invaluable in the context of responding and adapting to environmental pressures, including climate change-related displacement.

This article begins with a short overview of the discussion on terminology and regulation of mobility in the context of climate change, with particular reference to minorities and indigenous peoples. It goes on to elaborate in more detail specific (im)mobility scenarios that are associated with climate change, drawing out their specific relevance for minorities and indigenous communities. Finally, it outlines why minority and indigenous rights are an essential component, all too often overlooked, in the design and development of measures in response to climate change-related mobility.

1   IPCC, *Climate Change 2014: Impacts, Adaptation and Vulnerability – Part A: Global and Sectoral Aspects*, 2014, p. 12.
2   UNHRC, 'Human rights and climate change', Resolution adopted by the Human Rights Council on 22 June 2017, HRC 35th session.
3   OHCHR, 'OHCHR's key messages on human rights, climate change and migration'.

Overview of terminology, policies and legal status

Climate change-related mobility is a complex and disputed issue, with ongoing discussions around what the concept entails. Some terms, such as *climate- or environment-related migration*, suggest relatively 'voluntary' forms of movement while others, such as *climate or environmental displacement*, indicate forced movement. It should be stressed, however, that mobility in relation to climate change is taking place on a continuum between forced and voluntary migration, and the distinction between the two is rather blurred. The terminology and the 'nature' of the movement are not trivial issues, but have profound consequences for the legal status of affected persons, especially when crossing international borders. In addition, there are collectively organized forms of movement – the evacuation of communities following a natural disaster, for example, or their relocation in response to long-term environmental degradation such as inundation as a result of rising sea levels.

The political, public and academic debate on how to manage mobility in the context of climate change is also somewhat controversial. The global climate regime was initially very reluctant to include this issue within its regulatory framework: the 1992 UN Framework Convention on Climate Change (UNFCCC) is silent on migration in the context of climate change. Only the 2010 Cancun Agreement mentioned climate change-induced displacement, migration and planned relocations for the first time and called on states to take measures to enhance understanding and cooperation in this field. The 2015 Paris Agreement established a task force commissioned to develop recommendations for integrated approaches to avert, minimize and address climate change-related displacement. Besides a very small number of references to the rights and inclusion of indigenous peoples in the context of displacement related to adverse impacts of climate change, minorities and indigenous communities are not mentioned in the 2018 Report of the Task Force on Displacement.

One of the most substantial contributions to the discussion on legal responses concerning climate change-related mobility, in particular cross-border displacement, was the Nansen Initiative. Established with the aim of addressing the protection and assistance needs of persons displaced across borders, it was followed by the Platform on Disaster Displacement and resulted in the drafting of the Nansen Initiative Protection Agenda. This document defined three priority areas for action: collecting data and enhancing knowledge on cross-border disaster displacement; enhancing the use of humanitarian protection measures for cross-border disaster-displaced persons; and strengthening the management of disaster displacement risk in the country of origin. However, minorities and indigenous peoples were barely mentioned in the Protection Agenda.[4]

The Global Compact for Safe, Orderly and Regular Migration includes several paragraphs under the heading of 'Natural disasters, the adverse effects of climate change, and environmental degradation', and calls on states to 'develop coherent approaches to address the challenges of migration movements in the context of sudden-onset and slow-onset natural disasters'. Furthermore, the Compact emphasizes the protection of human rights related to, inter alia, members of ethnic and religious minorities and indigenous peoples in order to tackle and reduce vulnerabilities in migration.[5]

4   The Nansen Initiative, *Agenda for the Protection of Displaced Persons in the Context of Disasters and Climate Change*, vol. 1, December 2015.
5   UN General Assembly, *Global Compact for Safe, Orderly and Regular Migration*, Resolution adopted by the General Assembly on 19 December 2018, Article 23(b).

Most migration associated with climate change will take place within countries. Internally displaced people in a disaster situation have the right to be protected and assisted by the state in accordance with the state's obligations under international human rights law and international humanitarian law, where applicable. The UN Guiding Principles on Internal Displacement include 'natural or human made disaster' as reasons for displacement within a country. Principle 9 points out that 'States are under a particular obligation to protect against the displacement of indigenous peoples, minorities, peasants, pastoralists and other groups with a special dependency on and attachment to their lands.'

The legal status of persons displaced across international borders is not well defined and is precarious for those affected. International refugee law is applicable only in limited circumstances. Thus, the terms *climate refugees* and *environmental refugees* are in most cases legally inaccurate, and many international organizations and consultative processes, such as the Nansen Initiative, choose not to use these terms. However, members of minorities and indigenous communities displaced across international borders in disaster contexts may fulfil elements of the definition provided by the 1951 UN Convention relating to the Status of Refugees if, in situations of sudden- or slow-onset disasters, 'authorities deny any kind of assistance and protection to certain people because of their race, religion, nationality, membership of a particular social group or political opinion and as a consequence expose them to treatment amounting to persecution'.[6] In such cases, members of minorities and indigenous communities may be protected by international refugee law; however, in most other cases they may also be affected by the so-called

'normative protection gap', which refers to legal gaps in international law concerning the protection of persons displaced in a disaster situation across international borders.

Specific scenarios of (im)mobility, displacement and disruption

There are many migration scenarios that are discussed in the context of climate change. These are often associated with the specific cause of migration, such as the nature of a disaster or a climate impact driving movement. All of these scenarios are relevant and may pose particular challenges for minorities and indigenous peoples. This section provides an overview of some of the different environmental challenges that can contribute to migration or displacement, with particular reference to communities who may be especially exposed to these issues.

Sudden-onset disasters
Extreme sudden-onset events such as tropical storms and cyclones, heavy rains and floods are often associated with a clear link to displacement, although evidence suggests that migration responses after extreme events may also be quite diverse and multi-faceted. Every year considerably more people are displaced by natural disasters compared to displacements caused by conflict or wars. According to the Internal Displacement Monitoring Centre's (IDMC's) estimates, in 2018 16.1 million people were displaced by weather-related disasters such as storms, with Asia the worst affected of any region. In most cases, disasters lead to short-term, internal migration, but in some instances they can develop into longer situations of so-called 'protracted displacement'.

---

6   UNHCR, *Protecting People Crossing Borders in the Context of Climate Change Normative Gaps and Possible Approaches*, 2012, p. 32.

Migration as a consequence of sudden-onset disasters may also lead to forms of circular movements or even immobility. Although it might seem self-evident that people would leave a hazard zone when faced with an immediate environmental threat such as a flood or hurricane, they may also be unwilling or unable to move. Indeed, the costs of past displacement caused by earlier disasters may lead people to lack the resources to move again – a crucial issue for populations living in regions exposed to recurring extreme weather events.

Thus, the effect of sudden-onset disasters on migration is widely acknowledged as one of the most obvious and explicit scenarios in the context of climate change. There is, however, limited research on the specific context of religious, linguistic or ethnic minorities and indigenous communities with regard to displacement in the context of sudden-onset disasters. Besides some case studies, there are no figures or other systematic research available that would provide insights into the ways minorities and indigenous communities are specifically affected with regard to displacement in the context of sudden-onset disasters, although a broad variety of linguistic, ethnic and religious minorities and indigenous communities live in the regions most affected by disaster displacements, for example, in South and East Asia and the Pacific.

As mentioned, the significance of the social structure of the society, in particular issues of inequality, marginalization and discrimination, are crucial factors concerning the impact of climate change-related disasters, including on migration. Much of the impact of an environmental hazard is determined by the response of authorities and the ways this intersects with existing patterns of exclusion. Thus, the specific social, economic and political situation of minorities and indigenous people in a particular society is a crucial factor concerning the interrelation between a 'natural' disaster and displacement.

Marginalized communities often live in areas specifically exposed to impacts of climate change; they may be particularly dependent on and sensitive to changes in the ecosystem as well as the loss of livelihoods due to natural hazards and degradation; and they are typically affected disproportionately by poverty, which exacerbates the impacts of disasters. The case of Hurricane Katrina in the city of New Orleans in the United States (US), for example, constitutes one of the most scrutinized examples of the interrelationships between disaster, gender, age, ethnicity, poverty and (im)mobility. Neighbourhoods with a high proportion of black and poor residents were hit particularly hard by the floods inundating the city. A large number of inhabitants of New Orleans were not able to move out of the endangered city, most of whom belonged to the black, poorer, elderly as well as female population of the city. Furthermore, the state-led rescue and recovery services were accused by black residents of discrimination, with critics suggesting that the slow and poorly coordinated response by authorities was a product of racial discrimination.

Disaster situations affecting minorities, indigenous peoples and other marginalized groups illustrate how discrimination can deepen the impact on communities at every stage, with members not only exposed disproportionately to extreme weather events but also more likely to be excluded from humanitarian support in their aftermath. For example, Dalit communities in South Asia are repeatedly affected by devastating floods caused by weather-related or geophysical events such as monsoon rains or the 2004 tsunami. These recurring floods

cause considerable damage to housing and other possessions as well as the repeated displacement of thousands of Dalits. The tsunami in 2004 is reported to have displaced 650,000 Dalits in the southern Indian state of Tamil Nadu. Dalit communities are hit particularly hard because of their secondary social status: their homes are usually located on marginal lands on the periphery of settlements, where they survive on precarious livelihoods without legal rights to their land. Discrimination in access to relief systems, such as emergency shelters or the distribution of essential supplies, was reported after the 2004 tsunami and in subsequent monsoon floods. The International Dalit Solidarity Network (IDSN) has pointed out that humanitarian assistance tends to ignore caste dynamics and caste-related power

structures, thus exacerbating existing caste-based mechanisms of exclusion. In addition, this assistance fails to appreciate intersecting forms of discrimination, where caste-based discrimination interacts with gender, age, ability and other factors to put some Dalits at even greater risk.[7]

Another example is the growing number of wildfires in forested regions as a result of climate change, a development of particular concern for indigenous communities as well as minorities. It is projected that higher temperatures, longer droughts, dry soil and strong winds will provide favourable conditions for wildfires and increase their frequency, intensity and duration. That will, for example, be an increasing challenge for indigenous communities in Canada and the US as wildfires disproportionately threaten

7   IDSN, *Equality in Aid: Addressing Caste Discrimination in Humanitarian Response*, September 2013, p. 3.

their homes, living spaces and reserves. According to Todd Kuiack, the Emergency Management Director of Indigenous Services Canada, over the last 30 years the chance of being evacuated and displaced due to wildfires is 33 times higher for people living in First Nations reserves compared to people living off-reserve.[8] Displacements and evacuations as a result of wildfires have had profound negative consequences on the wellbeing of indigenous communities in Canada, resulting in social alienation, economic insecurity, limited access to education, poor mental health and other challenges.[9]

Slow-onset disasters and degradation of the environment
Long-term environmental change or slow-onset environmental degradation are caused by, among other issues, droughts and desertification, rising sea levels, melting permafrost and increased salinization of groundwater. These developments are considered to be an increasingly important factor in the context of migration. Migration patterns in the context of slow-onset events are diverse and context-specific, the interlinkages of climatic and other factors are still not well understood and the migration outcomes are difficult to project. The influence of slow-onset disasters on the decision to migrate very often is indirect and closely related to social and economic dimensions such as income, unemployment, access to education, potentially available migration networks and social relationships, poverty, inequality with regard to gender, ethnicity, sexual orientation, age and other categories. This scenario is often associated with varied forms of labour migration – internal or external, short-term, circular or permanent – in order to diversify income. Labour migration

is therefore used as a strategy to adapt to a changing climate.

The slow degradation of the environment due to climate change impacts poses profound challenges for minorities and indigenous peoples. In particular, minorities and indigenous communities living in rural areas who depend on natural resources for their livelihoods may increasingly find themselves in a position where migration either to urban spaces or even abroad is the only available option to diversify their income. In Palca, for example, a municipality in the Bolivian highlands with widespread poverty, a vast majority of the inhabitants live off agriculture. Some 90 per cent of the population self-identify as indigenous Aymara, a community largely residing in *campesino* communities governed by agrarian unions that exist alongside formal state structures and govern a range of social, economic and spiritual areas. Local households experience various pressures on their livelihoods, including social stresses such as land scarcity, market uncertainties and institutional marginalization, now exacerbated by water shortages, rising temperatures and an increase in rainfall intensity, hail and frost. With income from their agricultural activities dwindling and little in the way of alternative livelihood opportunities, community members are compelled to migrate to nearby cities or mines to work, often taking on poorly paid day labour. This migration, however, disrupts their family and community life and puts a greater strain on the remaining women, children and elderly to manage work at the farm.

This situation is far from unique. In order to tackle food insecurity and compensate for inadequate levels of family income

8   Yumagulova, L., 'Community resilience: connecting emergency management, education, infrastructure and economic development', *Haznet* 10(1), 2018.
9   Indigenous and Northern Affairs Canada and Laurier, *From Displacement to Hope: A Guide for Displaced Indigenous Communities and Host Communities*, 2017, p. 1.

An Aymara woman mashes potatoes to dry them under the sun in Chunavi village, Altiplano in Bolivia.

Panos / *Petrut Calinescu*

as a result of environmental change, indigenous people are often forced to search for work elsewhere, with many ending up in casual and insecure employment with few or no labour protections, low pay and hazardous conditions. Indigenous people may also face other challenges when moving into urban spaces, such as lack of access to adequate housing and other basic services, as well as discrimination against their traditional practices and way of life. This marginalization is especially acute for indigenous women. Climate change, for example, plays a significant role in driving urbanization in East Africa, where people are increasingly forced to move to towns and cities in search of livelihoods. These movements are reported to create female-headed households in urban and peri-urban areas who are forced to adopt multiple coping strategies in order to survive. Another climate change-related

movement scenario is the evacuation and relocation of entire communities, a last resort that some indigenous communities in, among other areas, Alaska, Louisiana and the Pacific Islands may be forced to adopt in response to sea level rise, erosion of coastal areas, extreme weather events and the thawing of permafrost. The so-called sinking Pacific island states, such as Samoa, Tuvalu or Kiribati, are widely discussed examples where a slow transformation of the environment is now threatening entire communities and even nations. Relocation processes have already begun, creating not only profound challenges for the relocated communities but also for governments responsible for carrying out these processes. Papua New Guinea, for example, started to relocate indigenous communities from the Carteret Islands and three other atolls to the larger neighbouring island of Bougainville. However, the relocation process has faced some profound challenges, including the identification of suitable land, disputes over land titles, limited political will to devote adequate resources to ensure success and insufficient livelihood opportunities for those relocated.[10] These obstacles have led to the creation of a community-driven initiative, Tulele Peisa ('Riding the Waves on Our Own'), which seeks to identify land and prepare a relocation plan with community involvement.

Similar relocation processes are either under discussion or already under way in the polar region, where numerous Arctic indigenous people reside. Their habitats across the Arctic, as well as traditional practices of hunting, harvesting and gathering food, are increasingly threatened by climate change impacts. Rising sea levels and coastal erosion are causing land loss in regions where Alaskan coastal villages are located. The Yup'ik village of Newtok, located near the Bering Sea in western Alaska with about 400 inhabitants, is a case in point: situated at a large river delta, it has been increasingly affected by erosion of the riverbank and degradation of the permafrost since the late 1980s. In turn, this has led to damaged infrastructure and contamination of the water supply. The inhabitants eventually decided to relocate to Nelson Island, several miles away from Newtok, and after land titles to the preferred relocation site were obtained a strategic relocation process followed. The process, however, progressed very slowly due to considerable local, state and federal legislative and institutional barriers. Recent reports indicate that some of the houses in the new village have now been constructed, with a planned completion date of 2023 for the resettlement of the community. But while relocation is sometimes the only option for Arctic communities in response to climate change impacts, indigenous peoples living in the region must also contend with added stressors related to oil, gas and mining activities, shifting land policies, pollution and a broader backdrop of poverty, exclusion and ill health.

Trapped populations, disruption of mobility patterns and voluntary immobility

The issue of 'trapped populations' refers to people who cannot move, even though the environment is deteriorating and posing a serious threat to their way of life, because they do not possess the means to do so. Climate change can increase the incentive to move, but also restrict their capacity to do so. Contrary to popular opinion, migrants rarely originate from the poorest parts of the population. Migration needs financial, social and other resources, and people may be forced to stay put because they cannot afford to move and face social barriers such as a lack of education, social networks or legal resources. Very often this poverty is manifest along indigenous, ethnic, religious, linguistic and other lines, including gender and age, as illustrated by the predicament mentioned earlier of residents in black and poorer neighbourhoods of New Orleans, who had no choice but to remain when Hurricane Katrina hit. Many of them were single mothers and older persons.

Climate change is also a factor that plays a role in the disruption of nomadic practices. The Sama-Bajau in South-east Asia refers to a number of sea-nomadic indigenous peoples living in Indonesia, Malaysia and the Philippines. The Sama-Bajau peoples' history and culture are strongly connected to the ocean, with communities traditionally depending on the sea for food, livelihoods and trade. Their nomadic lifestyle has been

---

10 Leckie, S., *Finding Land Solutions to Climate Displacement: A Challenge Like Few Others, Geneva*, Displacement Solutions, 2013, pp. 26–9.

undermined by many factors. Clearly defined national borders, government settlement programmes and restrictions on fishing grounds have put considerable pressure on their way of living. Climate change and the projected increase in frequency and intensity of extreme weather events are said to have further disrupted travel patterns as well as village life in the coastal zone. Other adverse impacts are expected from a loss of reef, seagrass and mangrove habitats, combined with challenges resulting from overfishing and other anthropogenic activities, which profoundly threaten the reefs in South-east Asia.

Nomadic herders in different regions of Africa have also been under increasing pressure due to recurring and intensifying droughts. Pastoralists normally move back and forth (transhumance) or from one place to another (nomadism) with their livestock to search for pasture and water. These practices have been influenced by many factors, including conflict, commercialization and now, increasingly, climate change. Due to intensifying droughts, the search for grazing areas in many countries has become more and more challenging, bringing nomadic communities into competition over land and water with sedentary populations, leaving animals without food and forcing some pastoralists to abandon their way of life altogether. These changes have far-reaching consequences, including challenges concerning gender roles. In Kenya, for example, the loss of livestock also means the loss of a man's social status and decision-making power. As many men are no longer able to pay a dowry to the bride's family in order to get married, this may cause a breakdown in family structures and a rise in the number of female-headed households.

Indigenous peoples may also choose to stay, even in the face of environmental deterioration or loss of their land, because of the deep cultural and spiritual connections they feel to their homeland. This is the case, for instance, among some communities in the Pacific: this 'voluntary immobility' can be understood as 'an important coping device, helping to strengthen cultural and spiritual agency among those facing the loss of their homeland'.[11]

Displacement, resettlement or eviction by climate change measures
Beyond its immediate impacts, climate change may also contribute to migration through other, less direct means. Notably, climate policies have been increasingly scrutinized in recent years with regard to their effect on human rights in general and forced movement of people in particular. In 2009, a report published by the Office of the UN High Commissioner for Human Rights (OHCHR) pointed out that climate-related activities such as mitigation and adaptation measures could have negative implications on human rights, such as the right to food or the rights of indigenous peoples, and could even lead to forced migration.[12] There have been numerous incidents of community displacement, resettlement or eviction as a result of land grabbing for the production of agro-fuels, renewable energy projects and even reforestation programmes funded by international climate mitigation instruments, such as the UN Programme on Reducing Emissions from Deforestation and Forest Degradation (REDD+).

Indigenous communities have been especially affected by many of these projects. The construction of hydropower plants, for instance, has repeatedly led

---

11 Farbotko, C., 'Voluntary immobility: indigenous voices in the Pacific', *Forced Migration Review* 57, February 2018.
12 OHCHR, Annual Report of the United Nations High Commissioner for Human Rights and Reports of the Office of the High Commissioner and the Secretary-General, Human Rights Council, 10th Session, 15 January 2009.

to the eviction of communities from their ancestral land. A case in point is Barro Blanco, a hydropower plant in the Province of Chiriquí, Western Panama, that in 2011 was approved under the Kyoto Protocol's Clean Development Mechanism (CDM) as a greenhouse gas emissions reduction project. From the outset, the project was met with strong opposition from the affected communities as well as from non-governmental organizations (NGOs), who complained that the development of the project infringed international human rights standards, in particular respect for the rights of indigenous peoples, by violating the right to free, prior and informed consent as recognized under the UN Declaration on the Rights of Indigenous Peoples (UNDRIP). It was argued that, in addition to the forced eviction of hundreds of members of the Ngöbe community, the project would have significant impacts on the natural resources of the communities affected. At the end of 2016, Panama formally withdrew the project from the CDM registry due to pressure from indigenous communities and international civil society organizations. Nevertheless, despite the protests and the filing of complaints at national courts and the complaints mechanisms of European financial institutions, the hydropower plant began operation in 2017. Barro Blanco vividly illustrates the risks that international development and climate policies can pose for indigenous communities, especially when implemented without complying with international standards or adequately applying safeguards to prevent displacement, eviction and other human rights violations.[13]

REDD+ has also been identified as a potential driver of indigenous displacement. As REDD+ aims to protect forests and reduce emissions from deforestation, the programme could potentially be beneficially to indigenous peoples, given their strong dependence on their surrounding environment and proven ability to manage these resources in a sustainable fashion. However, the OHCHR warned in 2009 that 'indigenous communities fear expropriation of their lands and displacement and have concerns about the current framework for REDD'.[14] From M'Baka in the Congo Basin to forest-dwelling Adivasi communities in India, REDD+ initiatives have been directly linked to the displacement or forced resettlement of numerous indigenous communities. While the advocacy of indigenous organizations and other NGOs helped push through the adoption of the so-called 'Cancun safeguards' in 2010, calling for the full and effective participation of relevant stakeholders, in particular indigenous peoples and local communities, in practice the implementation of these safeguards has proved problematic.[15]

Displacement in the context of climate change and violent conflict
Climate change is sometimes assumed to be a direct driver of conflict. Environmental degradation, increased food insecurity, economic insecurity, competition over natural resources and the rise of environmental hazards are all assumed to undermine human security and social cohesion, so increasing the possibility of violent conflict that could ultimately force people to migrate and flee their country of origin. However, it has been frequently emphasized that there is a lack of evidence of a direct link between climate change and violent conflict. Based on the review of academic literature and studies on this topic, the IPCC concluded that 'collectively the research does not

13 Hofbauer, J. and Mayrhofer, M., Panama *'Barro Blancho' Case Report*, COMCAD Working Paper 144, 2016.
14 OHCHR, *op. cit.*
15 HRC, 'Report of the Special Rapporteur on the rights of indigenous peoples', 36th session, 1 November 2017.

A Sama-Bajau fisherman swims to the surface with an octopus caught in the Banda Sea in Sulawesi, Indonesia.

Panos / *James Morgan*

conclude that there is a strong positive relationship between warming and armed conflict'.[16] Furthermore, the link between scarcity of resources as a consequence of climate-related impacts and conflict appears to be weak.[17] Indeed, climate change-associated impacts such as drought, storms and floods may even encourage the strengthening of solidarity mechanisms if communities and countries work together to support each other after a disaster. There are several factors, however, which can have a stabilizing or destabilizing effect in this context: the capacity of political institutions to facilitate adaptation and reduce vulnerability; education and preparedness; social capital such as neighbourhood networks

and cohesion; the availability of resources to support investment in resilience technologies and other adaptive measures; and whether or not the region has a prior history of conflict.[18]

In practice, then, it is perhaps more useful to view climate change as one element in a complex nexus of social, political and environmental forces that can, in certain conditions, contribute to a higher risk of conflict. One recent study, for instance, has argued that the risk of armed conflict is enhanced by climate-related disasters in ethnically fractionalized countries. However, the study does not find indications that environmental hazards themselves directly trigger

16 Adger, W.N., Pulhin, J.M. Barnett, J., Dabelko, G.D., Hovelsrud, G.K., Levy, M. et al., 'Human security', in *Climate Change 2014: Impacts, Adaptation, and Vulnerability. Part A: Global and Sectoral Aspects*, Contribution of Working Group II to the Fifth Assessment Report of the IPCC, 2014, p. 772.
17 Klomp, J. and Bulte, E., 'Climate change, weather shocks, and violent conflict: a critical look at the evidence', *Agricultural Economics* 44(1), 2013.
18 Burrows, K. and Kinney, P., 'Exploring the climate change, migration and conflict nexus', *International Journal of Environmental Research and Public Health* 13(4), 2016.

armed conflicts: rather, environmental hazards may act as a 'threat multiplier in several of the world's most conflict-prone regions'. Ethnic segregation in a broader context of political discrimination, economic inequality or poverty appears to play a significant role in this context.[19] Ethnic, social and political divisions can also prove decisive factors in the context of climate change, conflict and migration, as illustrated by the case of Typhoon Bopha and its impact in particular on the indigenous Lumad population. Having made landfall in the southern Philippines island of Mindanao on 4 December 2012, the typhoon caused severe and widespread damage and fatalities, with some 1,200 deaths and more than 1 million people left homeless. Subsequent rainfall that lasted for two months displaced a further 40,000 people. The impact of the typhoon was exacerbated by the fact that the region had been experiencing armed conflict between government forces and the National People's Army for several decades, with more than 100,000 people killed in the violence and thousands of others displaced. The conflict 'stunted the lives and opportunities for the Lumad population and contributed to an underlying vulnerability following the typhoon'.[20] Long-standing discrimination against the Lumad people hampered their access to economic and disaster relief. Shelters were established mostly in urban areas, forcing communities to move away from their rural homes, and were not built to accommodate indigenous needs and cultural traditions. Food and cash were only distributed to registered families, a requirement that many indigenous families did not meet, and the return to their ancestral land was jeopardized by the fact that the government established zones that were defined as unsafe to return to or to rebuild.[21] Mindanao illustrates how, in a broader context of discrimination and poverty, marginalized indigenous communities can end up locked in a cycle of displacement driven by natural resource exploitation, conflict and natural disasters.

Minority and indigenous rights, climate change and movement between regions

As discussed in this chapter, the interrelationship between climate change and migration is a complex and multi-faceted issue, requiring a comprehensive and many-layered response. Minorities and indigenous peoples, already occupying a precarious social, economic and political position in their countries, will likely face further human rights challenges in a context of climate change-related (im)mobility. It is therefore vital that a minority and indigenous rights perspective is mainstreamed into all climate change-related strategies. Disaster response systems, for example, which also manage displacement and evacuations, should ensure that at every phase of disaster management, from preparedness and early warning mechanisms to emergency relief distribution and reconstruction, minorities and indigenous peoples are not excluded – particularly those belonging to marginalized groups within those communities, including women, children, older persons and persons with disabilities. Of course, given that these mechanisms are informed by the broader rights framework in each country, it is necessary not only to integrate the principles of equality and non-discrimination in disaster response systems but also to

19 Schleussner, C., Donges, J., Donner, R.V. and Schellnhuber, H., 'Armed-conflict risks enhanced by climate-related disasters in ethnically fractionalized countries', PNAS 113(33), August 2016.
20 Bamforth, T., 'Social impact of Typhoon Bopha on indigenous communities, livelihoods, and conflict in Mindanao', in M. Companion (ed.), *Disaster's Impact on Livelihood and Cultural Survival*, Boca Raton, FL, Taylor & Francis, pp. 199–210.
21 *Ibid.*

combat inequalities and discrimination comprehensively through better access to education, health, housing, economic opportunities and justice.

Furthermore, the 2015 Paris Agreement has emphasized that states should respect, promote and consider their human rights obligations when taking action to address climate change. The protection of minority and indigenous rights constitutes an integral part of the human rights framework and, therefore, needs to be implemented in all climate response measures. This is especially pertinent when it comes to climate change-related movements between regions, for instance towards Europe and North America. Although the migration dynamics in the context of climate change and their relevance for movements towards Europe, for example, are still not well understood, and the data in this context is scarce, there is a common understanding that migration will predominantly occur within countries of origin and the consequences for migration towards Europe are highly uncertain.

However, that does not mean that there is no need for action by governments in the global North. Some people moving in the context of climate change, including members of minorities and indigenous communities, are already arriving in Europe, as the mention of climate-related factors such as drought in asylum applications in some European countries confirms. There is also evidence that increasing temperatures in countries of origin correspond with increasing asylum applications in Europe.[22] Similar reports have been made concerning the Americas, with extreme weather events such as the 1998 Hurricane Mitch in Central America believed to

have contributed to an upsurge in migration towards the US in the months following the disaster.[23] More recently, a succession of extreme droughts in Central America has been identified by some sources as one of many causes relevant to the 2018 migrant caravan moving from that region to the north.

In the absence of legally binding international law that comprehensively protects people displaced by disasters across international borders, existing human rights standards and, in conflict situations, humanitarian law have to be used effectively to protect the rights of those affected. In this context, a minority rights-based approach is important in two respects. First, while the extent to which members of minorities and indigenous communities are moving to Europe or North America in the context of climate change remains unclear, a minority and indigenous perspective is crucial to be able to address the particular needs of minority and indigenous members among refugee and migrant communities in Europe and North America, if necessary, and to optimally use and apply existing rights for the protection of minorities and indigenous peoples displaced towards Europe and North America. Second, a minority rights-based approach is also required in policies concerning refugee and migrant communities in Europe and North America as such (including for those for whom environmental reasons played a more or less crucial role), in order to promote social cohesion in receiving states. This includes the recognition of migrant identities, and the defence of the principles of non-discrimination and equality, as well as the fostering of intercultural dialogue and meaningful participation in all areas of society.[24]

22 Missirian, A. and Schlenker, W., 'Asylum applications respond to temperature fluctuations', *Science* 358(6370), December 2017.
23 Mahler, S., 'Central America: crossroads for the Americas', Migration Policy Institute, 1 April 2006.
24 For more on this, see Berry, S.E., *Mainstreaming a Minority Rights-based Approach to Refugee and Migrant Communities in Europe*, London, MRG, December 2017.

CASE STUDY

Kenya: 'There has been no life for us since we were moved out of the forest' – climate funding and the eviction of Sengwer from their ancestral lands

Hamimu Masudi

The indigenous Sengwer people, like other hunter-gatherer populations in Kenya, are living in constant threat of eviction from their ancestral lands in Embobut Forest. Classified as protected public forest by the colonial government in 1954, the community is now regarded by Kenyan authorities as illegal squatters, despite the fact that Sengwer have resided there for centuries and continue to depend on its resources for its food, livelihoods and cultural traditions.

In 2017, the African Court on Human and Peoples' Rights ruled in favour of the Ogiek indigenous people, against the government of Kenya in a land eviction dispute similar to that of the Sengwer population. The Court determined that in evicting the Ogiek community from the Mau Forest, the Kenyan government had violated the rights of the Ogiek to their ancestral lands. Much as this ruling should have set a precedent for other conservation projects, the Kenya Forest Service (KFS) continue to forcibly evict Sengwer inhabitants from the area, often violently, with hundreds of homes burnt to the ground since.

From colonialism to conservation – the danger of 'green' projects to indigenous Sengwer

The case of the Sengwer has attracted particular attention for being carried out in the name of conservation – and the complicity of international donors such as the World Bank in these abuses. Although the troubles of the Sengwer people began in the colonial era, when their lands were gazetted as forest reserves, in recent years climate funding has been singled out by the community as a major culprit behind the fresh wave of evictions.

Members of the Sengwer community protest their eviction from their ancestral lands in the Embobut Forest, by the government for forest conservation in western Kenya.

Reuters / *Katy Migiro*

'On the surface of it, the KFS guards stand to be blamed but this is only part of the story – there is a whole lot of climate funding that is so blind to human rights safeguards,' says Milka Chepkorir Kuto, a Sengwer female activist working to protect her community's land rights. 'Community complaints and independent expert findings have clearly shown that the plight of the Sengwer indigenous people is a result of a flawed approach to conservation.'

This is underpinned by longstanding accusations that Sengwer are responsible for deforestation in the area – a claim that Chepkorir points out is demonstrably untrue. 'We have lived many generations in the forest and have protected it,' she says, adding that deforestation is largely the result of new arrivals in the forest who carry out illegal logging and charcoal burning. 'The government seems not to see the difference.'

The World Bank's Inspection Panel, an independent accountability mechanism, was approached by Sengwer community members with complaints about the adverse effects of the World Bank-financed Natural Resources Management Project (NRMP), which ran from 2007 to 2013 in Mount Elgon, the Cherang'any Hills and other water catchment areas in the country. Reporting in 2014, the Panel criticized the project's implementation approaches for non-compliance with the World Bank's safeguard policies and failure to involve the community in the management of their forest resources, thereby creating conditions that led to evictions.

Another project, the EU-funded Water Towers Protection and Climate Change Mitigation and Adaptation project, has also attracted significant criticism for its contribution to the human rights violations against the community. In January 2018, following a spate of attacks by armed KFS guards on Sengwer activists, homes and livestock, three UN Special Rapporteurs issued a joint statement expressing their concerns about the plight of the Sengwer people as a result of project. Besides calling on the Kenyan government to immediately halt the evictions and conduct investigations into these abuses, it also called on the EU to suspend funding until steps had been taken to ensure indigenous rights were respected. Directly after their statement, a raid by the KFS left a Sengwer man dead and another injured, an action that prompted the EU to immediately suspend funding.

Living with eviction – the impact of resettlement on Sengwer residents

'Evictions have been affecting children from an early age, making it harder for girls to acquire the education that would help them recognize their legal rights, and develop alternative economic ways to provide for their families. Evictions not only affect Sengwer women, but also affect Sengwer girls, making them susceptible to harsh experiences and exposing them to situations where they are more vulnerable like getting into unions at an early marriage and most often with older men, thereby compromising their childhoods, and rights like education, play, reproductive health.'
- Milka Chepkorir Kuto

The brutal process of the KFS's forced evictions have been well documented, with thousands of Sengwer homes burnt to the ground, but these actions have also had a more intangible, longer lasting impact on their cultural and spiritual traditions. Milka has documented testimonies from a variety of affected community members in Embobut, Kapyego and Yatoi in Western Kenya that illustrate the wide ranging effects of evictions. From lack of access to medicinal herbs to early marriage, these are undermining the social fabric of the community and posing particular challenges for Sengwer women and girls. 'Evictions are disrupting the family as a social institution – men are deserting their families,' she explains. 'The clans and kinship system is being affected by distance, making it hard for people to adhere to the traditional norms that guide marriages and other traditional practices among the Sengwer community.'

The interviews she has gathered from fellow Sengwer testify to the heavy burden – social, economic, psychological – that displacement has exacted on communities. The loss of livelihood that many face after losing access to the forest forces community members to engage in poorly paid, insecure employment:

'Many live on other people's lands and work as a labourer to sustain their families. Life has become difficult for Sengwer women and their families. Previously, they used to have enough milk from their livestock to sell and consume, but now most children do not drink milk even weekly since their mothers are not settled and are unable to provide as much for them.' - Community member

The ever present possibility of eviction also creates greater uncertainty for community members in the forest, as well as the threat of intimidation and physical assault during the evictions. 'During evictions, verbal abuse and physical violence, including sexual violence, take place,' says Chepkorir. 'The women who experience these violations are not aware of the legal rights or mechanisms they could take in response to the violence.'

CASE STUDY: Kenya: 'There has been no life for us since we were moved out of the forest.'

Custodians of the forest

A sad irony of the treatment of Sengwer as a threat to nature is that, in reality, the exact opposite is true – given their dependence on the continued health of the local ecosystem and its resources, the community have a particular interest in maintaining the forest and have stewarded it sustainably for many generations. This is reinforced by their deep spiritual connection to the land. 'Sengwer women, just like every member of the community, cherish their culture,' says Milka. 'The community has sacred places in the forest where they perform their cultural rites and rituals.' This reinforces the pain of community members who have suffered displacement as many of these vital sites are now off limits.

Unlike, for example, the illegal loggers operating in the area, Sengwer are also careful to exploit natural resources in a sustainable fashion to ensure their continued productivity for many years to come. This is the case with their use of herbs for traditional medicines, a practice carried out for centuries by Sengwer women with care and respect. 'Generations have been taking herbs from the forest and glades for good health,' says one Sengwer woman. 'Women who go extracting and collecting herbs do not cut down a tree for herbs, but rather extract the specific part and leave the entire tree to continue growing.' Without access to these herbs, however, health issues among displaced Sengwer have increased.

'In our Sengwer culture, when was a woman even allowed to cut down a green tree? Why don't they just allow women and their children to go back and live in the glades? Our children are suffering from diseases they never suffered from when we lived in the forest; there are a lot of problems and bad health conditions. We would just like to be allowed to access our herbs, good and fresh air and clean water in the forest for our children and grandchildren. A woman is traditionally harmless to the trees. If they [KFS] claim they want to protect the trees, let the government therefore leave women out of evictions.' - Community member

A new approach

The heavy human cost of many large, top-down projects such as the donor-funded programmes in Embobut Forest point to the need for a new approach to climate and conservation projects on indigenous lands – one that not only respects, not disregards, the rights of the communities themselves but also engages them as equal partners in these efforts. The Kenyan government and international donors could, by upholding the rights of indigenous populations to their lands, also achieve significant environmental benefits by supporting tried and tested approaches to the management and preservation of natural resources. This would help promote sustainability effectively without sacrificing the needs of marginalized communities in the name of conservation.

'Do you think we should hope for the return of our ancestral land? Should we just agree with the government that we have left the forest as we negotiate for only grazing permission? Because these evictions and the loss they have caused us are becoming too much. But we still wonder where they want us to go together with our families, leaving our ancestors behind.' - Community member

Africa

Climate variability and weather extremes have posed challenges across Africa for generations and resulted in complex systems of indigenous knowledge around water management, land use and pastoralism that have ensured survival in the face of famine and other shocks. However, conflict, land grabbing and discriminatory policies have steadily undermined these traditional approaches, and now climate change is placing further pressures on communities.

While mitigation and adaptation are officially on the agenda in many countries, human rights violations against minority and indigenous populations persist – and all too often in the name of environmental protection. Kenya's indigenous Sengwer, for example, have faced eviction from their ancestral territories by the government with the supposed justification of protecting the forests they have stewarded for generations. There are now serious concerns that United Nations-sponsored initiatives to mitigate climate change, such as the UN Programme on Reducing Emissions from Deforestation and Forest Degradation (REDD+), could make their situation worse.

Pastoralist communities face different but no less significant challenges as unpredictable rainfall patterns, intensifying temperatures and desertification have disrupted seasonal migration cycles, placing greater pressure on water and land for grazing. In the process, this has deepened tensions with settled communities who depend on the same resources for agriculture and are themselves having to adapt to more extreme weather conditions. While some countries have taken steps to improve conditions through mediation and clear resource management frameworks, in other cases a long history of discrimination and institutional neglect towards nomadic and sedentary communities alike has meant that these issues have yet to be resolved. Without effective intervention, however, the risk of potential conflict could increase in future.

As elsewhere, climate change in Africa poses particular threats for excluded populations, including minorities and indigenous peoples, and marginalized groups such as women, children and people with disabilities. Recognizing and responding to these pressures is essential if existing inequalities are to be resolved rather than exacerbated in years to come. With food access and traditional livelihoods more precarious in an uncertain climate, human rights issues such as child marriage could become more prevalent among those communities hardest hit.

Africa: Introduction

Chad: As deserts spread south, pastoralists face scarcity and drought

Paige Jennings

A Toubou herder attends to his camels in the Ennedi Plateau, Chad. Panos / Frederic Courbet

Frequently ranked as one of the most vulnerable countries in the world to climate change, Chad has for years struggled with a range of environmental pressures that have also threatened its nomadic populations. Seasonal southerly migration by pastoralists and their cattle in the Sahel – traditionally in the dry season between October and May – has always caused friction with local sedentary populations reliant on the same pasture and wells used by herders to feed and water their livestock.

However, in recent years the impact of climate change has changed patterns in place for many generations, causing new tensions. Over the course of just a decade, landlocked Chad's dry northern Saharan and central Sahelian zones have spread 150 kilometres south, shrinking fertile farming and grazing areas. Decreasing or more erratic rainfall has forced herders – mostly Mbororo (Fulani, Peulh), Toubou or Gorane – to move south ever earlier in the year, with the result that at times their herds arrive before local farmers have had time to harvest their crops and spoil the yield. They also tend to stay for longer periods or even permanently, further upsetting the delicate balance between Chad's different ethnicities, lifestyles and livelihoods.

In the west, the shallow waters of Lake Chad, straddling the country's borders with Niger, Nigeria and Cameroon, have shrunk by an estimated 90 per cent since the 1960s, disrupting the routes and grazing patterns of livestock farmers from the countries around the lake. Closure of the Chad–Nigeria border since 2014 due to armed conflict hinders traditional trade and transhumance, forcing herders to sell more of their stock in Chad for a lower price.

The situation has been exacerbated by sparse and irregular rainfall across the Sahel region that has caused shortages of both fodder and water for pastoralist herds, forcing them south far sooner with serious consequences for animals and people. These include widespread food insecurity, disease outbreaks and economic difficulties, as well as increased risk of conflict with settled communities. In 2018, with 19 drought-affected departments declaring crisis or emergency phases in the 'lean season' from June to September – up from 17 the previous year – the situation left almost 1 million people in the region with little or no access to food.

These issues intersect with intercommunal tensions between herders and farmers in parts of Chad's eastern, southern and Lake regions, while the presence of refugees from conflicts in neighbouring Central African Republic (CAR), Sudan, Libya and

Nigeria has placed added pressure on limited resources in host areas. Exposure to armed conflict and banditry has also led to the proliferation of weapons: some northern herders have formed ethnicity-based self-defence militias to protect communities against theft and attack by other armed actors. Another complicating factor has been the emergence of some large 'neopastoralist' herds, run by professional drovers and said to be owned by wealthy and powerful Chadians. These groups have at times been accused of disregarding traditional regulations and the rights of local communities as they migrate south.

With almost 20 million head of livestock, pastoral farming accounts for between 15 and 20 per cent of the country's gross domestic product (GDP) and is said to contribute to the subsistence of around 40 per cent of the population. Historically, however, nomadic herders have had little political voice, though in recent years this has begun to change. Chad has been somewhat ahead of other countries in the region in attempting to mark and organize transhumance roads, set up agreed cattle resting and watering points and liaise with local residents and officials, with the aim of slowing the migration enough to give farmers along the route time to harvest their crops. Following a national conference in 2005 officials agreed to draft a new Pastoral Code, reflecting both farmer and herder input and including mechanisms for local conciliation of disputes, to replace the outdated and largely ignored 1959 version. Along with other countries in the region, Chad has also signed the 2013 Nouakchott Declaration on Pastoralism and the 2016 Bamako Declaration, both of which call for reinforcing the resilience of pastoral communities in the face of climate challenges.

On the ground, too, community organizations such as the Association des Femmes Peules Autochtones du Tchad (AFPAT, Association of Indigenous Peulh Women) are working with women, youth and children of local communities to establish alternative, sustainable livelihoods adapted to their changing setting. Emphasizing local approaches grounded in traditional knowledge, their activities demonstrate the value of participatory solutions that include pastoralists themselves – particularly as those are some of the communities worst affected by the changing climate. In the words of AFPAT's Hindou Oumarou Ibrahim, speaking at the April 2016 signing ceremony of the UN Paris Agreement:

'Our basic rights and our dignity are under threat. Climate change is adding poverty to poverty every day, and is forcing men to leave home, looking for a better future. Migration is challenging for rich countries, but it's a tragedy for those who are left behind, for those women and children who have to stay and fight back consequences of climate change on their own.'

'Our basic rights and our dignity are under threat. Climate change is adding poverty to poverty every day, and is forcing men to leave home, looking for a better future. Migration is challenging for rich countries, but it's a tragedy for those who are left behind, for those women and children who have to stay and fight back consequences of climate change on their own.'

In the west, the shallow waters of Lake Chad, straddling the country's borders with Niger, Nigeria and Cameroon, have shrunk by **an estimated 90 per cent since the 1960s,** disrupting the routes and grazing patterns of livestock farmers from the countries around the lake.

Chad: As deserts spread south, pastoralists face scarcity and drought

Kenya: For Turkana pastoralists, oil offers no easy solutions to poverty and drought

Nancy Omolo

A young Turkana herder stands in front of cows left under his supervision. Panos / *Frederic Courbet*

The Turkana people are traditionally pastoralists, a lifestyle adapted to the arid environments of north-western Kenya. Bordering Ethiopia, South Sudan to the north and Uganda to the west, Turkana County is the second largest of Kenya's 47 countries and covers some 77,000 square kilometres.

Turkana County is seriously affected by inter-ethnic and cross-border conflicts over natural resources. Turkana, like their neighbours, have a history of livestock raiding – a practice used as a means of extending grazing areas, securing control over new water sources and restocking herds with the livestock of enemy tribes. In addition to the cycle of retributive attacks this has generated, however, an additional challenge has been the transformation of raiding over the years into a more predatory or commercial activity.

Turkana, like other arid and semi-arid regions of Kenya, has a long history of marginalization from both the colonial and the post-colonial administrations. Due to prolonged isolation and under-investment, the region has some of the lowest levels of human development in Kenya and is the most prone to conflict and insecurity – a situation exacerbated by the recurrent droughts and unpredictable rainfall that have left communities even more vulnerable in their wake. Turkana community members also have limited access to education, elevated levels of health conditions such as child stunting and the highest incidence of poverty in the country. In this context, the ability to adapt to extreme weather and longer-term changes is crucial to maintaining traditional livelihoods in the region.

So far, Kenya has put in place a number of measures to mitigate drought and promote sustainable development. Following the National Climate Change Response Strategy (NCCRS) in 2010, outlining evidence of climate impacts on different economic sectors and proposing various adaptation responses, the National Climate Change Action Plan (NCCAP) of 2013 aimed to implement the 2010 NCCRS and set out a series of actions to enable low-carbon, climate-resilient development. The National Adaptation Plan (NAP) 2015–2030 builds on this by establishing adaptation priorities, while the Climate Change Act 2016 provides a regulatory framework for mainstreaming climate change considerations into development planning, budgeting and implementation across all sectors of government. Finally, the National Drought Management Authority Act

Kenya: For Turkana pastoralists, oil offers no easy solutions to poverty and drought

(2016) exercises overall coordination over all matters relating to drought management. Yet these measures have been hampered to an extent by delays and political obstacles.

In the meantime, Turkana County is currently undergoing major changes, including urbanization, population growth and shifting land use, that have put pressures on traditional nomadic lifestyles. Devolution, too, of significant levels of decision-making power to local authorities and increased central budgetary allocations to Turkana since 2013 to reduce the relative marginalization of the area have brought significant change. While a decade ago there were no commercial flights to Turkana, there are now at least five every week and in Lodwar, the largest urban centre, hotels and other forms of infrastructure have been built. This process of transformation could be accelerated even further by the recent discovery of vast oil deposits in the region. The reserves are currently being

explored by Tullow Oil, a multinational headquartered in London, with reports of more than a billion barrels available and projected investment of US$70 million by the company in 2019.

While some have welcomed the oil industry for the potential development opportunities it could bring the area, such as new road networks and employment for the local community, there has also been considerable resistance and concerns over the likely allocation of profits from any oil extracted, with prolonged demonstrations and roadblocks during 2018 in protest at the employment of outsiders over locals with the company. Given Turkana County's history of neglect, it is far from certain that oil revenues will be managed transparently and to the benefit of the region. Indeed, without effective participation and governance, the region's oil could make existing tensions even worse and lead to further conflict.

In this context, Turkana pastoralists face an uncertain future as increasing pressure on water, land and food security as a result of global warming has undermined their traditional livelihoods and generated conflict with other groups. A key element in maintaining stability and the survival of Turkana culture in the region is ensuring that the impoverished and excluded Turkana population have adequate access to food, services and other essential needs – in the process strengthening their resilience to climate change.

> The reserves are currently being explored by Tullow Oil, a multinational headquartered in London, with reports of more than a billion barrels available and projected investment of **US$70 million** by the company in 2019.

Kenya: 'The impact of climate change is worsening the situation of child marriage among the Maasai.'

A young Maasai girl with her family's goats. Alamy / *Ton Koene*

Nice Nailantei Leng'ete, a Maasai human rights activist and advocate for girls' rights in Africa, has saved thousands of girls from female genital mutilation (FGM) and child marriage through her work with Amref Health Africa, one of the foremost health rights non-governmental organizations (NGOs) in the region. She tells Hamimu Masudi about the effects that climate change is already having on Kenya's Maasai community and how young girls, in particular, are among the worst affected.

The Amboseli grasslands in Kenya and the Serengeti areas where the Maasai feed their cattle are all drying up – everyone is feeling the heat, the dry spells and the unpredictable rainfalls. When the rains eventually come, they are violent and cause a lot of damage to communities and to cattle. The droughts are widespread and longer, and as a consequence we lack grass to feed the cows – it is very common to see dead cattle all over the place.

Women and girls spend most of the day walking long distances in search of water, because the usual sources of water like rivers dry up often. And as a community that depends on cattle for our livelihood, the lack of pasture causes conflicts with crop growers, who complain of our cattle feeding on their crop fields. The pastoralists sometimes raid each other for grazing lands and cattle rustling. We also get media reports that snow on Mt Kilimanjaro and Mt Kenya is melting away, and we can imagine why floods have become so common. The elders say the nights are now colder and we see frost covering pastures, which is dangerous to the health of our livestock.

The impact of climate change is worsening the situation of child marriage among the Maasai. The prolonged droughts are forcing many families into desperate situations of hunger and young girls, as young as 12, are being given away as brides in exchange for cattle. The long walk in search of water also exposes young girls to the danger of sexual abuse and resulting pregnancies. As an activist for the girl child, I know this is happening, but it is difficult to gauge because of its underground nature.

The other serious issue is that, due to the cultural norms and values, girls who have undergone FGM attract a higher bride price compared to those who are uncut. It is also important to note that the girl who undergoes FGM is in essence being prepared for marriage, so the impact of climate change increases the risks of both child marriage and FGM. Indirectly, then, it can be argued that young Maasai girls are affected most by effects of climate change. A chronic drought and high costs of raising children all too often result in girls being viewed as an economic burden whose best place is a 'good' marriage.

The inability to predict the timing of dry and wet seasons greatly undermines our capacity to plan our risk preparedness and disaster management. But the Maasai are very resilient and adaptive to the effects of climate change. We are slowly but steadily venturing into other income-generating activities, like shoe making and business enterprises. In partnership with NGOs and churches, social campaigns and sensitization programmes are

also being conducted to fight child marriage and FGM. And through the support of organizations such as Amref, communities are being supported with irrigation and alternative livelihood projects like bee keeping and farming. These additional income sources help communities survive when it floods or when droughts destroy pasture.

As pastoralists, we are always on the move, so some families migrate to faraway places in search of pastures. Some go as far as Tanzania, or the slopes of Mt Kenya and Mt Elgon, but this is risky because it causes conflicts with farmers and other pastoralists. Last but not least, our traditional institutions – extended families, clans, the council of elders and the general community – help everyone through tough times.

The prolonged droughts are forcing many families into desperate situations of hunger and young girls, **as young as 12**, are being given away as brides in exchange for cattle.

Kenya: "The impact of climate change is worsening the situation of child marriage among the Maasai"

Namibia: Sharing local ecological knowledge through digital tools among the Ju|'hoansi

Megan Laws

Two rangers for the Nyae Nyae Conservancy test out a prototype for reporting incidents of poaching.
Megan Laws

The Ju|'hoansi of the Nyae Nyae Conservancy in northern Namibia are no strangers to climatic variability. In any given year, most families experience severe drought, wildfires and temperatures that drop to -2°C in the winter, then sudden flooding, dramatic thunderstorms and temperatures that soar to 38°C in the summer.

In the past, it was this seasonal cycle and not the months of the Gregorian calendar that marked a kuri 'year'. Today, these cycles appear to be getting longer. The heavy rains of summer are arriving later each year and the cold nights of winter feel more frequent than before. For the region's indigenous inhabitants, the stretching of seasons and the intensity of the drought, the variability of the rainfall and the extreme shifts in temperature are warning signs of climate change. These are also features of a semi-arid desert landscape that has long fluctuated between extended periods of drought and periods of relatively high rainfall.

Within the Namibian context, being able to discern between real, long-term threats to the region and what are long-standing patterns that the fauna and flora are well-adapted to endure and recover from are crucial to local livelihoods. As a 'conservancy', the region falls under the aegis of Ju|'hoan speakers. In Namibian legalese, they are the region's 'traditional community' – they recognize a common 'chief' or 'traditional authority', share the same

language, cultural heritage, customs and traditions, and inhabit the same communal area. While they are not its legal owners, they are the region's primary custodians and they hold ancestral rights to manage and utilize the resources found within it. These rights came into effect shortly after Namibia achieved independence from South Africa in 1990. By granting these rights to people living in Namibia's vast, rural landscapes, the aim was not only to achieve social-ecological sustainability but also to give people opportunities for economic development and political self-determination after decades of subjugation under the apartheid government of South Africa.

After years of community meetings and heated discussions, the Nyae Nyae Conservancy opted for a mixed subsistence economy of trophy and own-use hunting, foraging and harvesting, animal husbandry and agriculture, and research and tourism. The off-take is managed through a quota-based system, and the numbers for these are determined by a combination of aerial surveys,

Namibia: Sharing local ecological knowledge through digital tools among the Ju|'hoansi annual counts, and monitoring and reporting. These are undertaken by a team of rangers dispersed throughout the region and the environmental wardens and non-governmental organizations, such as the Nyae Nyae Development Foundation of Namibia, who work alongside them. It is an onerous task, and opinions are starkly divided between those who hail it as a conservation success story and those who claim that it is failing – in terms of both achieving social-ecological sustainability and economic development.

There is clear evidence of success. By securing grants, gathering research and film fees and supporting trophy-hunting and other commercial enterprises, the conservancy garners a large enough income to maintain solar-powered boreholes for 37 communities scattered throughout the 9,000 square kilometres region, distribute annual cash benefits to over 1,500 members and support numerous community projects, from small gardens to animal rearing and craft production. They remain the only indigenous community in southern Africa with both access to a large, ancestral territory and the rights to forage and hunt with traditional weapons. Their traditional n!ore land-use system continues to ensure the careful management of scarce resources, especially in times of drought.

Nevertheless, the situation remains challenging for many community members who still struggle with poverty and insecurity. Hunger is a daily battle for all but a few individuals with stable employment in town. A government feeding programme brings bags of maizemeal to destitute families throughout the year, but these alone are not enough to feed them. This pushes families towards town and into debt. An illegal invasion of cattle herders from the south is also threatening rangelands within the region, and poaching is increasing, both around the municipal town at the centre of the region and on the conservancy's borders. The distances between communities within the region are immense, making it difficult not only for residents and rangers to share local ecological knowledge and report their concerns, but also for relevant authorities and stakeholders to analyse and address these.

In 2015, to complement their ongoing efforts to achieve social-ecological sustainability and support communities through larger quotas, the Nyae Nyae Conservancy embarked on a new project to develop digital tools for expanding and streamlining monitoring and reporting. Working with Extreme Citizen Science, a research group at University College London, the conservancy designed two mobile applications for recording evidence of poaching and illegal grazing with the aim of using the data in an ongoing court case. These mobile applications were then expanded to support rangers to monitor and report back on animal sightings, and further applications designed for the purposes of mapping protected tree species or tracking regrowth rates in harvested plants. These applications are icon-based and therefore do not require high levels of print or digital literacy, and they allow rangers to record GPS coordinates that pinpoint immediate threats and areas of concern and support longer-term analysis and visualization of trends within the region.

The central aim of this work is to empower the wider community to voice their concerns and engage in the monitoring and reporting work that the conservancy depends upon. There are both technological and social challenges, however, that limit the extent to which these can complement current efforts. Poor telecommunications infrastructure prevents people from sharing knowledge quickly; having only minimal solar-power for electricity makes charging batteries a challenge, and, of course, only a handful of people have smartphones. Furthermore, only those who are formally paid to participate as rangers can, realistically, engage in monitoring and reporting work. Hunting and gathering is both risky and challenging, meaning people are increasingly pushed (as the local saying goes) to *zula ka ku |xoah*, 'roam in order to live' – to go back and forth from territory to town in search of work or patronage.

There are challenges, too, in establishing a clear and equitable interface between indigenous knowledge and new technologies. While the participatory design process employed with communities has meant that local people can both categorize and draw icons that make sense to them, not all local ecological knowledge is translatable in this way. It is also not clear what effect reification may have, and what new regimes of transparency these efforts may bring about.

Neighbouring communities face similar issues of environmental mismanagement and land encroachment that also impact upon local efforts to achieve social-ecological sustainability. As rangelands on the other side of the conservancy fence have been overgrazed, cattle herders have cut the fences into Nyae Nyae and allowed their cattle in to graze. Similarly, as deforestation has increased, either for logging or to make way for farming, so has the pressure from poachers who follow wildlife into the conservancy. While poor management and resource competition is driving this process, climate change heightens these impacts and brings new uncertainties. These are challenges that cannot be addressed simply through monitoring and reporting, but monitoring and reporting does, nevertheless, play a vital role. Current efforts to expand upon this work of drawing upon local ecological knowledge and bringing local people into the process, through both digital tools and broader forms of advocacy, are therefore important next steps. They mark a move towards gathering long-term, georeferenced data but also towards finding new ways to confront both a changing socio-political landscape and a changing climate. ◼

A hunter with his bow and arrow set in northern Nyae Nyae, Namibia. *Megan Laws*

Americas

Indigenous and Afro-descendant communities in Latin America have struggled for decades with the challenge of land rights violations by governments, companies and armed groups. These violations have often been accompanied by widespread environmental contamination and deforestation, with communal lands appropriated for mining, logging and plantations. The cost, in both human and environmental terms, has been extraordinarily high – hundreds of activists and community leaders killed every year, many others displaced and thousands of square kilometres of rainforest cleared.

Beyond the devastating impact of these abuses on the indigenous and Afro-descendant communities themselves, they also have profound implications for the global efforts to combat climate change, with deforestation in the Amazon in particular responsible for a significant share of global CO_2 emissions. According to a 2017 study, the Earth's tropical rainforests are now a net source of CO_2, with deforestation and degradation in the Amazon contributing nearly 60 per cent of emissions caused by human disturbance of tropical forest areas. As a result, the struggle for minority and indigenous peoples' rights in the region has become increasingly intertwined with efforts to curb climate change.

While communities have played a central role in mobilizing resistance movements, such as long-standing indigenous protests against land grabbing and forest clearance in Brazil – now taking on renewed urgency in the wake of President Jair Bolsonaro's rollback of environmental protections in the country – their contributions extend well beyond this. Indigenous concepts such as *Sumak Kawsay* ('good living'), for instance, with its emphasis on local, culturally appropriate, ecologically sound approaches to development and wellbeing, provide an important template for a more sustainable future. Indeed, while indigenous communities in the Americas are disproportionately affected by climate change impacts, given their reliance on surrounding ecosystems for food, income and spiritual meaning, their close knowledge of these precious resources and respect for nature also afford them considerable resilience. But while their adaptation strategies offer an important blueprint, it is crucial that traditional knowledge is not separated from a broader rights framework or treated simply as a product to be extracted from these communities without their consent or involvement.

The importance of climate justice, a response to climate change firmly rooted in human rights, is equally important in North America. Here indigenous peoples are also taking a stand to protect their lands from the construction of oil and gas pipelines that, beyond the immediate threats they pose to health and the environment, are also likely to contribute to climate change. Furthermore, minorities and indigenous peoples are among the first communities in North America to be displaced by climate change. Indigenous communities in Alaska and along the coast of the Gulf of Mexico are having to move because of rising sea levels and coastal erosion.

The disparity between those who contribute most to climate change and related problems such as air pollution, much of which is caused by the burning of fossil fuels, and those exposed to its effects reflects a broader context of inequality between different ethnic groups. In the United States, a recent study found that on average non-Hispanic white populations were exposed to 17 per cent less air pollution than they produced, while African Americans and Hispanics suffered a 'pollution burden' 56 per cent and 63 per cent higher respectively than they generated through their own consumption. The study focused on the emission of fine particulate matter (PM2.5), which is largely caused by human activity, especially the burning of fossil fuels – a major contributor to climate change. The authors emphasized that their 'pollution inequity' metric is also generalizable to other pollution types.

Canada: 'Some people say it's going to be indigenous people to stop climate change, but it will take every single person, not just indigenous people.'

Members of the Tiny House Warriors campaign at work. Photo supplied by Kanahus Manuel.

Kanahus Manuel is an indigenous activist, author, birth keeper and founding member of the environmental indigenous activist group Tiny House Warriors – a protest movement against extractive industries on indigenous territories. She explains to Alicia Kroemer how indigenous communities, particularly women and youth, have been at the forefront of environmental resistance – and the important contribution they are now making to the fight against climate change.

I am Kanahus Manuel. My name means Red Woman in Tanaka. I am from both Secwepemc nation and Tanaka nation – they border each other on the Rocky Mountains on the west coast of British Columbia in Canada. The Secwepemc territory is still to date unceded and unsurrendered. There are 10,000 Secwepemc living there. It is a very rare temperate inland rainforest.

The landscapes, geography and biodiversity make up so much of who we are. Everything we are is from the land. With indigenous communities, it always comes back to the land. We have been able to sustain ourselves for thousands of years. We have place names in our language that are as ancient as the mountains around us. We have a close relationship to and dependence on our land, unbroken since the beginning of time.

Right now, one of the biggest threats to our land and livelihood is industry, as it has always been. Resource extraction, in the form of pipelines, logging and mining, continues to threaten our people. Here in Canada we are currently facing threats of unconsented resource extraction and destructive access into our territories with expansion of roads and pipelines. Today, the Canadian government is trying to build the Kinder Morgan/Trans Mountain Pipeline on Secwepemc territory, and they now own the company, which they bought for C$4.5 billion in 2018 from Kinder Morgan, a Texas-based company.

This Trans Mountain Pipeline threatens thousands of clean glacier creeks, streams and lakes. It is a bitumen pipeline. Bitumen is toxic; it is not conventional oil, you cannot clean it up with conventional oil spill methods – it sinks. This is why we bring attention to it and connect it with some of the big mining disasters we've had in the past. We have seen first-hand that government and corporations do not invest enough into cleaning up environmental disasters from these projects. They never cleaned up the Mount Polley mine disaster that happened in our territory in 2014, they just covered it up. The toxins of that disaster are continuing to spill into one of the deepest glacier-fed lakes in the world, Quesnel Lake.

'Right now, one of the biggest threats to our land and livelihood is industry, as it has always been. Resource extraction, in the form of pipelines, logging and mining, continues to threaten our people.'

Kanahus Manuel

We look ahead to the next 10,000 years. If our ancestors have been here for 10,000 years and we are still able to drink from the glacier-fed streams today, what do we have to do to ensure 10,000 more years of clean water for future generations? Right now, our glaciers are receding at a rapid rate all around the world. What will it look like when our glaciers are gone? What will that look like for humanity?

In protest against this violence on our land and communities, we have started the Tiny House Warriors movement. The Canadian government has always displaced us from our land, yet we have always been mobile. We have currently set up tiny houses on wheels at Blue River, stopping 'man camps,' which bring in hundreds of Trans Mountain Pipeline male construction workers. In addition to the environmental destruction of resource extraction, the presence of 'man camps' brings with it an increase in sexual attacks and violence towards indigenous women, contributing to the reports of missing and murdered indigenous women. The increase in violence towards women has occurred near similar camps in northern British Colombia, northern Alberta and North Dakota. This is why we chose to put our tiny houses first on the ground here at this site this past year.

We need people on the ground. The power that indigenous people have is often found in their leaving the reserve. I am telling them to leave that little prison and exercise rights on all territories and stop resource extraction. Some people say it's going to be indigenous peoples who stop climate change, but it will take every single person, not just indigenous people. It is going to take every single one of us on this planet. To the non-indigenous world, I say to you: this is your government; this is your history of colonialization and oppression. You need to take

Kanahus Manuel, founding member of environmental indigenous activist group 'Tiny House Warriors.' Photo supplied by Kanahus Manuel.

'We are not going to let the old boys' club and rich people around the world continue to control and destroy the planet. We are the masses that are waking up to climate change, and the urgency is now.'

/ *Kanahus Manuel*

responsibility and fight back for protection of the lands and water.

Today we see a movement happening in our indigenous nations, that it is the women who are standing up. An indigenous woman started the Standing Rock Protest. Indigenous women have initiated the healing from the violence of colonialism. It is through this healing that the women found their voice to stand up to our oppressors, against state and extractive industries. The women are beginning to find their voice and the men are beginning to stand by their side as our indigenous communities heal.

Indigenous youth hold vast potential power – they are the ones who have the warrior spirit. They are young and able bodied, they are able to be out there on the frontlines, they have artistic minds that can be creative in finding new ways to resist. Indigenous youth have such a huge job on their hands and it's going to take that creativity and youthful spirit to be able to make change. Indigenous youth can change the world. Once they find their voice, there is a ripple effect and we

will continue to see more indigenous people coming to the forefront and speaking out against climate change and protecting our Earth. These young people are bringing us into a new era – a new generation of resistance.

Every day, we are striving to become the independent, strong, thriving indigenous nation that we envision. But this is going to take work at each individual level. We are not going to let the old boys' club and rich people around the world continue to control and destroy the planet. We are the masses that are waking up to climate change, and the urgency is now. I encourage everyone to start thinking and planning for solutions. I call on indigenous communities around the world to pull away from dependence on colonial states. We saw people standing up around the world for Standing Rock, standing up against destructive extractive industries. It's going to continue. Follow the voices of the indigenous women and youth as they lead us. We are empowered by protest, both indigenous and non-indigenous, to fight for our lands and water to ensure our future survival.

Ecuador: Indigenous communities lead the fight against climate change and oil extraction on their land

Karleen Jones West and Todd A. Eisenstadt

In the centre of Ecuador's Amazon forests, the Kichwa people of the Pastaza River watershed village of Sarayaku have worked to document how climate change affects their community and their livelihood. In June 2012, two generations of Sarayaku's indigenous leaders – José Gualinga and Marlon Santi – travelled to Quito to meet with scientists at the Pontificia Universidad Católica del Ecuador (PUCE).

Portrait of Patricia Gualinga, an indigenous rights defender of the Pueblo Kichwa de Sarayaku, an indigenous community in the Ecuadorian Amazon. ©*Amazon Watch*

Seeking greater ties between some of Ecuador's leading Earth scientists and indigenous communities, Sarayaku's leaders wanted to measure climate change on the ground to improve Kichwa environmental stewardship and ensure their adaptability.

As a belief system, indigenous cosmovision regards nature as an essential component of humanity. Yet unlike many Western belief systems – including some religions and political ideologies – it is compatible with and complemented by the philosophy of science. In Ecuador, indigenous peoples are harnessing their knowledge of Pachamama – Mother Nature – and finding scientific support for ancestral traditions, all in an effort to protect their lands from a changing climate.

Furthermore, indigenous communities in Ecuador recognize the role that global capitalism plays in creating climate change. Some indigenous leaders argue that the rejection of capitalist production and consumption are necessary not only to protect indigenous traditions, but also to sustain the Earth for future generations. As Sapara leader Ricardo Ushigua explained, 'For us there is no capitalism. Everything is collectivism. Anyone can harvest what they want, and the land belongs to everyone.' He further added that money was not important to his people. Rather, what mattered was 'living well with the richness of the Earth'. Indeed, to Ushigua, the pursuit of monetary wealth and living in harmony with the environment were almost incompatible.

Other indigenous communities regard globalization as an opportunity to pursue sustainable development. Pasqual Callera, Economic Development Director for the Achuar People of Ecuador's southern Amazon, observed that the self-sufficiency of his community in the era of climate change depends on finding environmentally sound ways to engage with global markets. For example, the Achuar community have pursued ecotourism through the Hotel Kapawi, a rainforest lodge they have operated for over a decade. 'Our plan,' Callera explained, 'is to develop alternative technologies which do not pollute, to show it can be done that way.' In addition, Achuar leaders agreed that international allies were necessary to pursue their mission of ecotourism and sustainable development. For example, with help from Norwegian engineers, Callera hopes to develop solar-powered canoes that facilitate transportation through Amazonian tributaries without the pollution produced by petroleum-powered motors.

In 2008, Ecuador seemed poised to be a leader in establishing environmental protections as a way to prevent climate change. Under the leadership of then-President Rafael Correa, Ecuador ratified the first Constitution in the world that gave Mother Nature rights. Then, Correa publicly agreed to protect the biodiverse rainforest of Yasuní National Park from imminent oil drilling, recognizing that the Amazonian region contains the 'lungs of the world' and is essential to stop global warming. However, his agreement came with one crucial caveat: international donors would have to pay Ecuador to offset the oil revenues the country would forgo by leaving the oil in the ground. After collecting a few million US dollars – only a fraction of the funds sought – the Correa administration decided in the summer of 2013 to discontinue the campaign and drill for oil in the National Park.

Correa's policies had devastating consequences for many indigenous peoples in Ecuador. Oil extraction was pursued not only in Yasuní – where several Waorani communities live in isolation from the Ecuadorian state – but deeper into indigenous territory throughout the Amazonian region. Ironically, Correa justified his policies by co-opting an element of Kichwa cosmovision known as *Sumak Kawsay* – which in Kichwa means 'harmonious living'. What was once a phrase that the Kichwa people and other indigenous communities had used to represent the bond between humanity, nature, spirituality and responsibility for future generations was instead subsumed into the contradictory agenda of the Correa administration. By 2014, many indigenous and environmental groups were distancing themselves from the philosophy of *Sumak Kawsay* as a vision for preventing climate change or trying to make the distinction between the government's attempt to coopt it and its original intent.

Sarayaku Kichwa continue to be leaders in promoting the rights of indigenous peoples in the face of climate change, not just in Ecuador, but around the world. Winning a case in the Inter-American Court of Human Rights in 2012, the Sarayaku Kichwa not only successfully prevented the Ecuadorian government from extracting oil on their lands, but they also reinforced the international norm of 'free, prior, and informed consent', which requires states to consult meaningfully with indigenous communities regarding any policy or activity that directly affects them.

Recognizing the direct relationship between the pursuit of oil and worsening climate change, in 2015, Sarayaku leaders brought their 'Canoe of Life' 6,000 miles from the Amazon to Paris to demand international climate action as part of the United Nations Framework Convention on Climate Change. Three years later, in August 2018, Sarayaku launched their *Kawsak Sacha* – or Living Forest – proposal, which, among other things, argues that 13 million hectares of living forest are destroyed annually, that fossil fuels are the primary factor destroying the environment and that the most affected communities are the world's indigenous peoples. Their project demands that the Ecuadorian government preserve and protect the territories that provide for the material and spiritual wellbeing of the Living Forest – the home of indigenous peoples.

To view the Sarayaku proposal and express your solidarity with their vision, visit https://kawsaksacha.org/. For more information on Ecuador's extractive policies, indigenous responses and climate change, read Who Speaks for Nature? Indigenous Movements, Public Opinion and the Petro-State in Ecuador *by Todd A. Eisenstadt and Karleen Jones West.*

Ecuador: Indigenous communities lead the fight against climate change and oil extraction on their land

Panama: The devastating cost of 'green' development for the indigenous Ngäbe-Buglé community

Jaume Rius Lopez

Guaymi are the most numerous indigenous people in Panama. They are also known by the name Ngäbe and are closely affiliated with a small group known as Buglé. They traditionally live in the western provinces of Bocas del Toro, Veraguas and Chiriquí, though many have migrated to other parts of Panama in search of employment.

Most Ngäbe-Buglé live in small rainforest settlements and identify with their communities more directly than with their ethnicity, which in turn affects their level of national political organization.

The Ngäbe-Buglé organized in the later twentieth century to protect their land and culture. Their society was disrupted by the spread of banana plantations, the construction of the Inter-American Highway through their territory and the appropriation of their communal lands by mestizo peasants and cattle ranchers.

The 1972 Constitution required the Panamanian government to establish *comarcas* or reserves for indigenous communities, but this policy was not universally implemented. After years of protest, in 1997 the Ngäbe-Buglé were finally granted their own *comarca*. Nevertheless, the erosion of their land rights caused many to leave and join Panama's migrant workforce, where they were generally given the lowest paid and most physically challenging jobs.

An indigenous Ngäbe Buglé woman stands at a distance from the Barro Blanco dam in the Chiriqui, Panama. *Agustin Abad,* www.agustinabad.com.ar

Inadequate social services continue to be the major issue in the remote areas where Ngäbe-Buglé settlements are located. Although the Panamanian government has expressly committed itself to children's rights and welfare, these benefits often do not reach Ngäbe-Buglé areas. Indigenous children are not always able to attend school due to financial and economic constraints, lack of schools or transportation and insufficient government resources.

In the country's sugar, coffee and banana plantations, Ngäbe-Buglé continue to work under worse conditions than their non-indigenous counterparts. Migrant Ngäbe-Buglé families leave their isolated settlements in search of income. During the harvest of sugar cane, coffee, bananas, melons and tomatoes, farm owners often pay according to the volume harvested, leading many Ngäbe-Buglé labourers to bring their young children to the fields to help with the work.

Like other indigenous communities in Panama, they have also had to contend with land rights violations. The most recent instance of this included a highly controversial hydroelectric project known as 'Barro Blanco'. This project was first proposed by then-President Martín Torrijos and was championed by his successor, President Ricardo Martinelli, as a means for the country to improve its energy security through green energy sources. The project was subsequently registered in the United Nations (UN)-sponsored Clean Development Mechanism (CDM), a financing tool set up in the wake of the Kyoto Protocol to support climate adaptation by providing development projects with the opportunity to claim credits based on the estimated volume of CO_2 offset. Following this approval, the project subsequently received US$50 million in additional funding from European investment banks.

However, the project attracted increasing international condemnation amid reports that the project was approved without the free, prior and informed consent of the affected Ngäbe-Buglé community, who stood to lose their entire way of life. In particular, the project was strongly criticized by the Special Rapporteur on the rights of indigenous peoples, James Anaya, in 2014. The controversy eventually resulted in the Panamanian government formally withdrawing the project from the CDM in November 2016. However, despite the community's opposition to the completion of the dam, in December 2016 Panama's Supreme Court ruled in favour of the project, deeming Barro Blanco a matter of 'public interest'.

The project illustrates the potential pitfalls of many international environmental financing mechanisms, such as CDM and UN Programme on Reducing Emissions from Deforestation and Forest Degradation (REDD+), if large-scale projects are implemented without adequate consultation with local communities. Though the Ngäbe-Buglé are not the only indigenous people to have suffered displacement, loss of livelihoods and other impacts as a result of development programmes supposedly intended to reduce climate change impacts, the human and environmental costs to the community have been devastating. Since the flooding of the river, crops have been destroyed and the area plagued by mosquitoes. The project has led to the flooding of Ngäbe-Buglé homes. Sacred petroglyphs that have traditionally been worshipped during an annual Ngäbe-Buglé pilgrimage have also been submerged under the waters of the dam. In May 2018, the Tabasará River was drained for dam maintenance work, wiping out local fish stocks and leaving many Ngäbe-Buglé with no source of protein. Their case highlights the importance of ensuring that any investments in climate resilience respect the rights of indigenous communities and are undertaken only with their full consent.

This profile is an edited version of the community profile featured in the Panama country entry of MRG's World Directory of Minorities and Indigenous Peoples.

Peru: Hunger and malnutrition among Shawi communities in the Amazon

Carol Zavaleta

While Peru has enjoyed a protracted economic boom, the situation for many of its indigenous communities remains challenging. Indeed, in some areas of the Peruvian Amazon, food security and nutrition are more strained than ever as development projects, deforestation and rapid population growth have increased pressure on local resources.

However, these issues have become even more pronounced as the effects of climate change – including rising temperatures, more intense flooding and severe droughts that disrupt the fragile hydrological system – are increasingly being felt.

The Armanayacu watershed is located in the Amazonian region of Loreto, in the north of Peru, and is home to 19 Shawi indigenous communities with a total population of over 1,000 inhabitants. Situated in high jungle, where altitudes range between 120 and 800 metres above sea level, temperatures are high all year round and precipitation is constant, although there is a significant decrease in rainfall between April and October. Despite residing in one of the most biodiverse regions in the world, however, Shawi households have been struggling to maintain an adequate and nutritious diet. Consequently, these communities now find themselves on the frontline of the climate change impacts threatening the Amazon ecosystem.

Shawi community members have themselves highlighted how conditions appear to have become much more variable in their territory, with at least four major incidents of flooding reported by the local disaster risk management authorities between 2015 and 2018. The impact of these events has been considerable. For instance, during one serious flood that took place in November 2017 the water rose half a metre and remained at that level for around five hours. While there were no casualties, the secondary school was severely affected, with the library, furniture and educational material largely destroyed. Major flooding events have often forced the school to remain closed for prolonged periods until it is safe again for the students to return.

In particular, climate change is undermining access to local food resources, with serious implications for Shawi community members. Some report having to skip meals and even not eat for a whole day because they are not able to find enough game or fish to meet their needs. This sort of scarcity was far less common in the past. In one of the most distant communities, one older Shawi remembers when his father arrived for the very first time at the Armanayacu River, at the beginning of the twentieth century, when animals were abundant in the forest. According to an older Shawi woman, 'In the past, you used to feel hunger only when you were not able to go to the forest. Women could hunt fish easily in the river – these days I do not know what my grandchildren are going to eat.'

Shawi report that around 30 years ago, they used to spend a couple of hours at most hunting deer, huangana and sajino (two varieties of peccary) and

majás (a paca or large rodent). 'These days,' says one community member, 'we go to the forest with hunger, and return bringing more hunger.'

Climate change also represents a challenge to Shawi agriculture, since many households have turned from hunting and gathering food from the forest to rely more on working the land and growing crops to eat or sell. The market for these goods, however, is limited by the low price assigned to many Shawi crops, such as corn and plantain, in Yurimaguas city. Higher temperatures and a less predictable rainy season could further impair these activities and undermine crop production.

However, the community has developed some effective coping strategies that may provide a measure of resilience to the challenges of climate change. For example, groups of Shawi males will together go into the forest and spend several nights there before returning with whatever they are able to catch – often just one small monkey – to share among their relatives. It is a common practice among Shawi to share food, especially when hunted or gathered from the forest, and this is one of the main strategies developed by Shawi to overcome food insecurity and meet the food needs of those community members, such as older persons, single women and couples that have recently had a child, potentially at risk.

There are also new challenges, beyond climate change. While the region has now become more accessible, with the construction of a new road that has facilitated the arrival of outsiders to the area and an accompanying sharp rise in levels of deforestation, the implications for indigenous communities and their food security remain uncertain. In recent years, the increasing presence of many non-Shawi people as owners of new grocery stores has resulted in processed food, such as soft drinks and alcoholic beverages, becoming much more widely available, with greater chances of developing other forms of malnutrition such as obesity and chronic health conditions. In addition, the road is used by large trucks to transport wood throughout the year, while in the past wood was only transported by river and mainly during the wet season. Far from improving access to nutritious food supplies, the road could – by accelerating population growth,

fragmenting the forest with construction and scaring away animals from the area with the noise – further diminish the chances of finding meat and fish in the region. In addition, the high level of food insecurity forces some Shawi to engage in activities that put at risk the survival of the fragile ecosystem. For example, some households have had to sell wood to illegal loggers in order to access cash to buy supplies for their children's education.

In this context, education is one potential pathway to improve food security in the future. Given their strong social cohesion, Shawi believe the benefits of education would

Members of a Shawi community in Peru. Indigenous Health Adaptation to Climate Change (IHACC) / *Matthew King*

extend beyond individual students to the entire community. 'With high education levels,' says one resident, 'we know he or she will share. When the youth have an income they will share with their family – Shawi are like this. The future is education; an NGO [non-governmental organization] or the government must support knowledge for agriculture production, then each family will have their incomes and be fine.' Shawi are therefore keen to see improved educational access alongside the preservation of indigenous knowledge and adaptive strategies. This means that authorities need to respect the local vision of economic development and build on existing indigenous social institutions, such as the traditional customs surrounding the sharing of food and income, to strengthen household food security.

The impact of climate change on Shawi communities needs to be understood in a broader context of discrimination and exclusion. Peru's indigenous communities have long struggled with poor food and nutritional access, and their dependence on local flora and fauna for their survival makes them especially vulnerable to environmental pressures. While longitudinal data for Shawi communities is not yet available, food security among indigenous people in the Peruvian Amazon appears to be getting worse, despite the country's rapid economic growth:

one study, published in 2015, found that levels of chronic malnutrition among indigenous children were as high as 56 per cent compared to 22 per cent among non-indigenous children.

Despite the reliance of Shawi and other Amazonian indigenous communities on locally farmed and forest food sources, the response of the Peruvian government has typically been oriented towards the delivery of non-indigenous and processed food products through school or municipal programmes, with limited attention being paid to the voices of Shawi themselves. While Peru published its Framework Law no. 30754 on Climate Change in 2018, representative bodies such as AIDESEP (the Interethnic Association for the Development of the Peruvian Rainforest) are calling for indigenous perspectives on food security and diet to be incorporated into the new law. Measures such as these, reflecting indigenous food preferences and livelihood needs, could help generate a more equitable form of development that includes indigenous peoples in the Peruvian Amazon.

This case study draws on research conducted as part of the Indigenous Health and Adaptation to Climate Change Research Program (IHACC), a multi-year project in the Peruvian Amazon, Canadian Arctic and Uganda examining the health impacts of climate change on indigenous communities.

United States: Hurricane Katrina hit minorities in New Orleans hardest – and without effective intervention the next disaster will do so again

Lisa Overton

Almost 14 years on, New Orleans is still recovering from the devastation wrought by Hurricane Katrina in August 2005. Causing unprecedented economic damage and bringing an entire city to a standstill, without access to infrastructure or basic services, Katrina represented one of the worst natural disasters in the history of the United States (US).

However, it did not happen in a vacuum. As well as revealing stark inequalities, particularly across race and class, Katrina was the catalyst in a multiple- and prolonged-impact event that included a number of storm surges and multiple levee breaches from the two rivers that engulfed New Orleans as well as a chemical explosion and massive oil spill, ending with another hurricane, Hurricane Rita.

As such, it illustrates the complex intersection of climate change with wider institutional failure and discrimination. Its unequal impacts and fraught aftermath demonstrate the need for an intersectional approach to disaster prevention and response that recognizes and addresses inequalities, particularly those experienced by minority populations.

Vulnerabilities, climate change and federal failure

Katrina occurred at a time where there was a lot of debate about climate change, and for many observers it appeared to confirm the worst. Nevertheless, at first there was little 'concrete' data to prove a correlation between the rise in global temperatures and the destructive intensity of Katrina, with only one study emerging a year

22-year old Tammy sits on a piece of junk on a derelict street. She was made homeless by Hurricane Katrina which hit New Orleans, Louisiana in August 2005.

Panos / *Robin Hammond*

later that proposed that Katrina's impact was intensified due to a rise in ocean temperatures. Since then, however, with a growth in specialist technology, there is more evidence to suggest that hurricanes can indeed be worsened by climate change, with a range of research demonstrating that storms such as Katrina are likely to have been exacerbated as a result.

Though the debate is ongoing, it is widely accepted that temperatures had risen at the time and have continued to rise ever since, while hurricanes are intensified by warmer sea temperatures. At the same time, the destruction of the mangroves along the Gulf Coast and land subsidence have removed natural protections from storm surges. All this suggests that climate change and environmental pressures are likely to have increased the risk of a natural disaster such as Katrina. However, it is not just climate change that is the issue

here, but also the social and economic disparities of New Orleans itself, with its minority populations among those worst affected because many were less likely to have the resources to adapt and more likely to be living in unsafe and more exposed conditions.

Minorities at risk

In the 1990s, disaster scholars drew attention to the fact that minority populations can be rendered more vulnerable than mainstream populations after a disaster and through this work led disaster research towards greater recognition of the social forces that could turn a natural hazard into a disaster. The catastrophic after-effects of Katrina illustrate this point. While few were untouched by Katrina – from the upper-class neighbourhoods of Uptown, to the artistic, 'hipster' areas of MidCity, to the projects of the Ninth Ward – pre-existing power relations around position in society, access to resources and distribution of income mean that some communities were less well placed to recover than others. Disasters can thus be seen as social events that reveal the inequalities, vulnerabilities and coping mechanisms that inform how people negotiate the 'permanent disaster' of daily life.

After Katrina hit the city, thousands fled to the Superdrome sports stadium where the authorities were meant to be providing protection, shelter, supplies and care. But they were completely underprepared and supplies, including fresh water, ran out in days. Where minority identities intersected, the impacts of Katrina were especially acute. Among African-American New Orleanians, for example, research showed that working-class identity and gender could exacerbate the impacts, with women at the centre of this intersection disproportionately affected by Katrina. This reality was explained through the fact that African-American women are more highly concentrated than any other demographic in services and sales, with already lower job security and wages than other areas of employment and in industries that were slow to recover post-Katrina. What are also revealed here are the implications of pre-existing inequalities faced by minority populations. To put this into context, around the time of Katrina, only 14 per cent of African-American women in New Orleans aged 25 and over had degrees, compared to 55 per cent among their white and Hispanic counterparts. This is despite the fact that over half the population in New Orleans is African-American.

Furthermore, some members of the Hispanic New Orleanian population faced the additional burden of documentation where their prior status was not legal. This prevented some segments of Latinx New Orleanians from being able to access vital resources and federal support, including access to temporary living space, food stamps and emergency funds. This situation persisted post-Katrina, when it was reported that many reconstruction workers were Latinx but employed on precarious contracts that meant they were not being properly paid and their labour exploited – a situation that was exacerbated when workers did not have official documents to prove their visa status. There were also language barriers for those who were relatively new to the United States, making it difficult to negotiate 'red tape' such as complex form-filling.

The worst affected were those who were already vulnerable due to lack of access to resources to evacuate out of state and due to where in the city they lived, with poorer neighbourhoods situated on lower-lying ground, as well as how they were treated by officials in recovery and reconstruction. As indicated above, where minority identities intersected, the impacts of Katrina could be worsened: research has also shown that disabled people, elderly people, particularly women, linguistic minorities such as Cajun and Creole people, as well as indigenous peoples, faced a greater impact as a result of Katrina. For instance, while New Orleans is hailed as the 'gay capital of the South' and as such has a higher population of LGBTQ+ people, the state of Louisiana in general is not known for its tolerance to queer sexualities. Research by New Orleanian scholar Charlotte D'Ooge about lesbian women's experience post-Katrina found that lesbian women struggled to gain access to relief services and found their relationships were not recognized by officials, demonstrating that lesbian identity and relationships placed them in a position of vulnerability and discrimination.

The effects of Katrina were exacerbated by the state's failure to maintain infrastructure or address pre-existing inequalities. Had the investments been made to improve the levee systems, had a proper evacuation plan been in place, had the mangroves been restored, Katrina would never have happened the way it did. This reveals the complex intersection of climate change with institutional responsibility and, moreover, how inseparable institutional commitment to infrastructure is from climate environments, locally and globally.

Improving security in the context of a changing climate

While research on the connection between the increasing frequency and intensity of hurricanes and climate change is still ongoing, based on the available evidence there is good reason to be concerned about the implications of rising temperatures and other impacts for New Orleans and similarly exposed cities. With research indicating that hurricane intensity is deepening and little evidence that a suitable levee system is now in place, should another hurricane make its way to New Orleans it is very possible that the city will again experience disaster. Though better evacuation procedures are in place, in the event of further destruction it may not be possible for many people to return, and this does not account for those who are still not able to evacuate due to a lack of economic and social resources to do so.

This reflects not only the reality of a changing climate but also the limited commitment of the state to investing in adaptation infrastructure.

Katrina occurred during the Bush administration, whose official line was to deny climate change, and as the violence and bloodshed of the Iraq conflict was escalating further. The so-called 'war on terror' took precedence over natural disaster public spending, which included the maintenance of infrastructure in a city that was home to a large population of minorities who were disproportionately affected as a result. At the same time, it should be highlighted that these vulnerable populations were and are much more than victims. In many cases, they have existing strategies and coping mechanisms in place that, with proper investment and support, could protect them and their communities from future shocks. The challenge, however, is implementation when access to resources and representation remains so restricted.

More fundamentally, the inequalities that shaped the way the disaster of Katrina unfolded in 2005 remain largely unchanged today, with New Orleans recently ranked as the second most unequal city in the country. These divisions, too, are still evident along ethnic lines, with incomes in 2016 of just US$25,800 among African-American households in New Orleans compared to US$64,400 for white households. Little research exists about further intersections among minority groups such as Creole, Cajun and Latinx peoples or queer communities. This is worrying, given that climate change research suggests that disasters will only intensify in future – and that minorities, as vulnerability scholars have highlighted, will be the worst affected. ■

Asia and Oceania

Asia and Oceania are among the areas of the world most vulnerable to climate change, with a large proportion of its populations located in coastal areas that are especially sensitive to rising sea levels and frequent natural disasters, including extreme weather events. The vast water towers of the Tibetan plateau and its adjacent mountain ranges feed the Indus, Ganges, Brahmaputra, Yangtze and Yellow Rivers, upon which 1.4 billion people depend.

Snow and ice reserves have for millennia been crucial to ensuring relatively stable and sustainable access to water. By disrupting snow and rainfall as well as accelerating glacial melt, climate change will affect water availability and food security; the Brahmaputra and Indus river basins have been identified as particularly vulnerable to reduced flows.

Climate change is also having a severe impact in the Pacific, where indigenous populations in countries such as Kiribati and Tuvalu are now confronted with the possibility that much of their territory could become uninhabitable in the near future. Already, flooding and other environmental impacts have forced thousands to relocate from their homes to safer areas. In a broader context of declining livelihood opportunities and widespread poverty, climate change is further exacerbating a pattern of large-scale migration from many Pacific countries. The cost of this disruption to cultural traditions, spiritual practices and local languages is immeasurable.

In Australia, Aborigine and Torres Strait Islander communities are mourning the loss of vast sections of the Great Barrier Reef to large-scale bleaching, especially in 2016 and 2017. Coral bleaching has been linked to rising water temperatures. A recent study has revealed that the coral is struggling to recover; the number of new corals settling on the reef has declined by 89 per cent since those bleaching events. Coastal indigenous communities depend on the reef for its natural resources and to uphold cultural, spiritual and social values. Australia is regularly experiencing intense heatwaves, badly affecting various forms of wildlife that are struggling to cope. Millions of fish died in the Murray-Darling River basin in three massive kill events in early 2019 as a result of the drought and water mismanagement. Hundreds of Aborigine activists demonstrated in March, calling for greater indigenous involvement in managing the river system. Local Aboriginal community members emphasized that what had happened was not only an ecological disaster but a profound cultural one as well.

Communities in the region are struggling with climate change impacts that frequently reinforce existing patterns of discrimination. Marginalized minorities such as South Asia's Dalits, who survive precariously on local resources and are often excluded from what limited institutional support systems may be available at times of crop failure or drought, are particularly exposed to these impacts as a result. In turn, these pressures can contribute to the steady flow of Dalit migrants from rural areas into cities, where they frequently occupy environmentally hazardous, unserviced areas on the urban periphery. As with other minority and indigenous communities, discrimination shapes their experience of climate change at every stage: this is why Dalit activists have called on governments to integrate a rights-based approach to adaptation to ensure the most vulnerable groups are included.

Climate change also intersects with mining, deforestation and energy projects across the region that not only contribute to global warming through their generation of greenhouse emissions, but in the process devastate the forests, lakes and mangroves on which many communities depend. From the destruction of Indonesia's rainforests for palm plantations to the disruption of the Mekong River by hydropower dams, the environmental stress brought on by this development is exacerbated by climate change – and minorities and indigenous peoples are disproportionately affected. While communities have initially mobilized in response to the immediate impacts of these developments on their local environments, the broader framework of climate change resistance has also provided them with a powerful platform to broadcast their human and environmental cost.

Australia: As the Great Barrier Reef shrinks, Torres Strait Islanders have everything to lose

Jaume Rius Lopez

The Melanesian Torres Strait Islanders have lived on the islands north of Queensland for at least 10,000 years and are closely related to the nearby Papuan people of Papua New Guinea. Because of their marginal location, Torres Strait Islanders largely escaped the early excesses of European invasion and settlement until well into the nineteenth century, when a pearling and trading economy began to develop.

In the twentieth century there was considerable migration to the Cape York peninsula on the mainland and to the large urban centres of Cairns, Townsville and Brisbane. Today there are approximately 32,500 Torres Strait Islanders in Australia and another 26,600 with both Aboriginal and Torres Strait Islander heritage. Approximately 7,000 people live in the Torres Strait, with just over 4,000 people residing in the Torres Strait Island Region, the main local government entity that was created in 2008. The majority are indigenous: nearly 65 per cent of the population in the Torres Strait Island Region are Torres Strait Islanders and just over 8 per cent are Australian Aborigines. The majority of the Torres Strait population is increasingly concentrated in the urban centre of Thursday Island. The inner islands just north of Cape York are the traditional home of the Kaurareg Aboriginal people.

Following a long campaign for recognition of their land rights, beginning in the early 1980s, in 1992 the High Court upheld the claim. There were also campaigns for self-government, driven in part by the perceived neglect of the federal and

A boy with
a fish spear
walks along
an ineffective
seawall on
Saibai Island,
Australia.

Alamy /
Suzanne Long

Queensland state governments, and
greater powers were subsequently
devolved to the Island Councils and
the Torres Strait Regional Authority
(TSRA), established in 1994.

The contemporary economy is
based on fishing, but much of the
population is dependent on welfare
services. Islanders have experienced
discrimination and inadequate access to
employment and services. Land issues
have also posed problems. Compared
to the rest of the country, Torres Strait
Islanders continue to experience
high levels of poverty and exclusion.
For example, while in the country as
a whole 31 per cent of homes are
owned outright and only 30.9 per cent
rented, on the Torres Strait Islands

just 3.1 per cent are owned outright
and the large majority (91.7 per cent)
are rented. Together with Australia's
Aboriginal population, Torres Strait
Islanders also face far poorer health
outcomes, with a gap of almost 11 years
in life expectancy between indigenous
and non-indigenous Australians.

Now climate change is creating further
challenges for the community. Rising
sea levels, strong unpredictable winds,
coastal erosion and high tides have
become increasingly evident in the
Torres Strait. In some areas, the impacts
are already being acutely felt. In 2012,
sacred sites and the cemetery on
Saibai Island were flooded by very
high tides. On Boigu Island, which
is the northernmost community in

Australia, the cemetery was threatened by flooding in July 2017 and sections of road washed away into the sea. These two islands are especially vulnerable and are facing inundation by high tides on an annual basis. The communities living on these islands are settled on smaller areas of land between the sea and swampy ground in the middle of the islands. Higher tides add to the water levels inland as well as along the seafronts. In February 2018, Yam Island was also hit, with king tides destroying houses and possessions, leaving families homeless. Salt water compounds the issues facing the communities, contaminating the groundwater and soil. Disasters like these will become increasingly commonplace in the years to come. According to the TSRA, sea levels are rising by between 6 and 8 mm every year, more than double the global average of 3.2 mm, in turn damaging the fragile marine and coastal ecosystems on which the way of life of thousands of Torrent Strait Islanders depends.

The heavy environmental toll of climate change is especially acute in the Great Barrier Reef. Torres Strait Islanders, together with Australian Aborigines, are the traditional owners of this unique natural asset, with much of their culture and traditional livelihoods built around its rich ecosystem. In the last few decades, however, its corals have been steadily dying. Recent estimates point to the alarming fact that the northern section of the Great Barrier Reef had already lost more than half of its coral cover since 2016. While pollution and an accompanying explosion in the number of starfish has contributed significantly to the reduction of the coral reef, bleaching from heatwaves is also a major factor – with climate

change a major culprit in the increasing intensity of these extreme temperatures.

In combination with persistent coastal erosion and inundation, many island communities may eventually be forced to relocate unless significant investments in flood protection are made across the islands in the near future. Given the fundamental role that land and sea play in their identity, the impact of such a move on the wellbeing of Torres Strait Islanders could prove devastating. In the words of Getano Lui, deputy mayor of Torres Strait Island Regional Council: 'What is instilled in us and our ancestors is if the Torres Strait sinks, we'll sink with it.'

This profile is an edited version of the community profile featured in the Australia country entry of MRG's World Directory of Minorities and Indigenous Peoples.

According to the TSRA, sea levels are rising by between **6 and 8 mm** every year, **more than double the global average of 3.2 mm,** in turn damaging the fragile marine and coastal ecosystems on which the way of life of thousands of Torrent Strait Islanders depends.

Thailand: For Thepa's Pattani Bay community, a coal-fired power plant could bring an entire way of life to an end – and in the process accelerate climate change across the planet

Nicole Girard

'Just living is not enough.
I must have fresh air and freedom.'

—Thepa protest sign

Thepa is a small minority Muslim village in Thailand's southern province of Songkhla, nestled in Pattani Bay. Its people rely heavily for their livelihood on the sea and the coastline, with its mudflats and mangrove forests that are natural fish nurseries. Estuaries run from the Sankalakhiri mountain range, contributing to the bay's rich biodiversity. Coconut, durian and watermelon groves supplement their fishery activities.

Thepa is part of the former sultanate of Patani that existed before it was annexed by the British to Thailand in 1902. It remains a contested zone to this day, where violence has simmered between those fighting for independence and the Thai state. Tensions run deep between the central Thai administration, relentless in the face of decades of failed assimilationist and centralizing policies, and the local Muslim populace.

When Thailand's state-owned Electricity Generating Authority of Thailand (EGAT) proposed a coal-fired power plant and nearby deep sea port in Thepa in 2014, the locals were immediately concerned. More than 200 families were set to be evicted with no clear plans for relocation or restitution, while mosques, Islamic schools, graveyards, houses and agricultural land were also located within the proposed area. Many were aware that such a project would not only destroy their community and way of life, but also lead to further violence from the independence movement and a heavy-handed response from Thai security forces.

Plans for the Thepa power plant, along with its twin plant in Krabi, are in stark contrast to the Thai administration's international commitments, particularly those made in its Intended Nationally Determined Contribution (INDC), under the Paris Agreement. A report, submitted in 2016, notes that as 'a developing country highly vulnerable to the impacts of climate change,' it intended to 'reduce its greenhouse gas emissions by 20 per cent from the projected business-as-usual (BAU) level by 2030.' Nothing is mentioned, however, about its plans to build coal-fired power plants in pristine coastal areas.

'The Thai government always has two-faced politics', explains Dr. Supat Hasuwannakit, director of Green South Foundation (GSF), a local environmental civil society organization (CSO), and doctor at the nearby Chana Hospital for the last 20 years. 'One face is a strong country moving toward Sustainable Development Goal (SDG) commitments in the international platform; the other is at national platforms, where the Thai government is always reluctant to work hard toward their commitments because industrial groups are strong in Thailand. They have a very close relationship, so it is not easy to reduce CO_2 and greenhouse gases to implement their climate commitments.'

The planned 2,200-Megawatt (MW) Thepa plant will be constructed in an area of 4.5 square kilometres and is just one of a total of six new coal-fired electricity-generating plants proposed by EGAT to be completed by 2025. EGAT governor Kornrasit Pakchotanon asserted that EGAT needed to be the market leader and the power plants were the means by which to achieve this goal.

Despite the significant risks this development posed to local communities whose culture and livelihoods depended on the sea, consultations with residents were deeply flawed. An Environmental Health Impact Assessment (EHIA) was privately commissioned by EGAT in 2014. Community members who opposed the project were not allowed to participate in the public review. Coils of razor wire surrounded the venue for the hearing, and the governor of Songkhla province sent 1,500 troops and police to prevent

The planned 2,200-Megawatt (MW) Thepa plant will be constructed in an area of **4.5 square kilometres** and is just **one of a total of six** new coal-fired electricity-generating plants proposed by EGAT to be completed by 2025.

Thailand: For Thepa's Pattani Bay community, a coal-fired power plant could bring an entire way of life to an end...

A report, submitted in 2016, notes that as 'a developing country highly vulnerable to the impacts of climate change,' it intended to 'reduce its greenhouse gas emissions by **20 per cent** from the projected business-as-usual (BAU) level by 2030.'

following continued repression by Thai authorities to prevent public gatherings, 17 activists were arrested and charged with violating this junta order.

In February 2018, community members continued their resistance with protests in Bangkok, organizing outside the Government House and subsequently undertaking hunger strikes. In response, the Ministry of Energy announced that plans for the Thepa and Krabi plants would be postponed for three years. Shortly afterwards, the ministry signed an agreement to undertake a Strategic Environmental Assessment (SEA) to assess the appropriateness of coal-fired power in southern Thailand. GSF continued to pressure the Ministry of Energy to ensure that the government body responsible for the SEA would not be one that is aligned with the pro-coal movement. The National Institute of Development Administration (NIDA) is now responsible for the study.

GSF and the wider anti-coal network are collaborating with the SEA process and support the selection of NIDA, which they believe will approach the study from a neutral standpoint. Following public hearings in April and May, the process is set to be completed by August 2019 – a timeframe that some community activists consider rushed. While the postponement of the project was a short-term victory for the coal resistance movement, many doubt that the project will be shelved entirely. According to Hasuwannakit, 'we're still not convinced that plans for southern coal are really gone since the SEA process is still ongoing, plus southern coal is also in the 20-year National Strategy Plan by the government.

any villagers opposed to the project from gaining access. The junta administration even issued an order with the intention of speeding up construction by removing certain procedural safeguards and checks.

GSF, along with a local community group known as the Network of Songkhla-Pattani People Against Coal, initiated a sustained non-violent community resistance campaign. A series of monthly forums were held to increase public solidarity, increase community knowledge relating to the power plant and climate change impacts and give training to community teams that would assist with community-led EHIAs. Bringing together a wide range of different groups, including women and youth, the wider network began organizing peaceful protests, with demonstrators dressed in green calling for an immediate halt to the power plant. In December 2017,

Moreover, the Energy Ministry plans to bid out 8.3GW of new independent power plants (IPPs) which in international news they mention using coal as fuel but in Thai news, they don't mention coal.' For activists with experience in challenging state-imposed development projects in the region, this lack of transparency raises serious concerns.

Importantly, while rooted in resistance to the clear and immediate danger that the plant poses to the health, livelihoods and wellbeing of the local community, the protests have evolved to take on the larger consideration of climate change at a national and global level, with the certain damage that further coal plant construction would bring through added CO_2 emissions giving an added impetus to activists and demonstrators. 'The locals,' says Hasuwannakit, 'know very well about the negative impact of the coal-fired power plant to their community. Yet they also now understand the connection to climate change at a basic level. They are proud that their Thepa group is part of the global movement fighting climate change.'

'The locals know very well about the negative impact of the coal-fired power plant to their community. Yet they also now understand the connection to climate change at a basic level. They are proud that their Thepa group is part of the global movement fighting climate change.'

Dr. Supat Hasuwannakit

Thailand: For Thepa's Pattani Bay community, a coal-fired power plant could bring an entire way of life to an end...

Tibet: Nomads caught between climate change and government 'conservation'

Gabriel Lafitte

A Tibetan nomad walks her yaks up a hill. Panos / *Kieran Dodds*

The impacts of climate change on the Tibetan Plateau – melting glaciers, river runoff, rising lakes and increasing rainfall – are well known. Yet the impacts on Tibetans themselves, numbering some 6 million people and occupying almost 2 per cent of the planet's land, attract far less attention. Instead the focus is almost entirely geopolitical, on global impacts and global responses: actual Tibetan land managers are absent, even though they make land-use decisions daily in a climate that has always been highly variable, requiring great skill in living with uncertainty.

First, the bigger picture. The glacial sources of Asia's great rivers, at 6,000 to 8,000 metres above sea level, overlooking the vast Tibetan Plateau, are melting fast. Despite some initial confusion within the Intergovernmental Panel on Climate Change (IPCC) as to the likely rate of ice loss, there is now no disputing the accelerating mass imbalance. Similarly, the overtopping of the lakes and heightened river flows are by now all well documented, especially in Chinese scientific publications.

This is where the consensus stops. Although Tibet is the most inhabited of cryospheres, it is also out of bounds to international media and human rights activists. As a result, the experiences of local communities at the frontline of climate change are neither heard nor acknowledged. In the absence of Tibetan voices, the significance of rapid warming is argued by states, scientists and geoengineers, all seeking global results.

For China, short of water for industry, agribusiness and urbanization, increased runoff is a dividend;

likewise the prospect of a coming climate more able to support crops and forest species familiar to lowland China. Water provision from Tibet has become the top priority for China's central planners, resulting in the zoning of prime grassland landscapes as national parks from which most Tibetan pastoralists are excluded, in the name of guaranteeing water retention and downstream provision. This is part of the Chinese government's strategy to control the hundreds of thousands of square kilometres of alpine meadow between the glaciers and lowland China, which the Yellow and Yangtze Rivers flow through. Ultimately, the official policy is to return huge areas to their original, pristine state as grassland wilderness, ignoring millennia of landscape curation by nomadic herders.

China's dividend of increased river flows due to glacier melt will turn to deficit when the glaciers are gone. That will take most of this century, it seems, far away enough for little immediate concern, and perhaps compensated for by increasing precipitation. For thousands of years, lake levels across

Tibet have been slowly falling, as monsoon rains reaching into Tibet from the Bay of Bengal through the Himalayas have steadily reduced in intensity. Now, especially in the land of lakes of northern Tibet, that trend has reversed. The summer of 2018 was one of the wettest known in Tibet, and Chinese scientists now worry about lakes breaking their banks and flooding far below.

China's water dividend from Tibet will be locked in legislatively in 2020, when a chain of national parks will be formally launched, including the Sanjiangyuan, or Three-River Source National Nature Reserve, in which all human presence, from mineral extraction to nomadic pastoralism, is categorized as a threat to be excluded. Further enhancement of the water dividend is planned by geoengineers who propose cloud seeding the Sanjiangyuan catchment, triggering precipitation by firing rockets laden with silver iodide at monsoon clouds drifting in from distant oceans. However, it is far from certain that the enthusiasts for geo-engineering, on a scale never seen before, can demonstrate that their technologies are effective, especially at a time when rain is already increasing due to climate change.

Beyond China, glacier melt generates much alarm, yet so far little attention has been paid to the Tibetan lives and livelihoods being removed and shut out in the name of climate change adaptation. China's desire to recreate 'original ecology' in depopulated Tibetan landscapes is explicitly intended to grow more grass and increase biomass by excluding grazing animals, thus capturing carbon and

in the process earning China – the planet's biggest emitter of carbon – accolades and global carbon credits.

Minority and indigenous populations worldwide face pressure from ranchers and plantation growers who want their land, but seldom on such a scale, and in the name not of palm oil and beef but of climate change mitigation. Conservationists who would be expected to welcome a declaration of protected areas will, in 2020, have to carefully consider the declaration of the Sanjiang, Qilian and Panda National Parks, and the exclusion of local Tibetan customary guardians from their lands.

On the ground in Tibet, for both pastoralists and crop-growing farmers, climate change affects everything. Much of the Tibetan Plateau – an area the size of Western Europe – is a permafrost zone, but the permafrost itself is now melting fast, which not only releases methane into the atmosphere but also drains away frozen soil water into the deeper earth, beyond the reach of young grasses and sown crops. The early arrival of spring, months before the summer rains arrive, is now a problematic period, with temperatures suited to growth but on lands that have not in the past required irrigation.

Permafrost melt greatly affects the many wetlands of Tibet, drying them out in spring before the summer rains arrive, in the process compromising habitat for migratory species. As in many areas worldwide, the climate change trend is for more extreme weather. In Tibet, long prone to intense gales and blizzards, this means more sudden hailstorms destroying the ripening crops of barley farmers, and more livestock herds trapped behind snowed-in high passes, perishing because they cannot reach lower grazing grounds. China does not provide insurance schemes for such disasters, relying instead on relief campaigns led by cadres. Meanwhile, in Tibet's wetter and warmer south-east, habitats change as one ascends any mountain, from subtropical to alpine, on a single slope, creating many habitats suited to varied species of plants and animals. As the climate is warming rapidly, however, there is not enough time for them to adapt and go upslope.

In many Tibetan areas, official policy changes require dryland upland farmers to convert much of their farmland to trees, or to close farms altogether, without effective reforestation. This is known as 'grain to green' and the 'sloping land conversion program'. China has not employed local Tibetan communities to re-forest areas logged intensively for decades. Young trees on exposed slopes, lacking the protective canopy cover of older trees, are extremely vulnerable to frosts. All of this exacerbates the precariousness of Tibetan lives, with Tibetan children already prone to undernourishment.

Tibetans who speak publicly of such issues are seldom tolerated in a highly centralized system where only official voices are permitted. Although Tibetan non-governmental organizations (NGOs) have discreetly worked to help local communities adapt to climate change, high-profile environmentalists are criminalized and imprisoned. This effectively removes Tibetans from the public sphere, excluding them from any opportunity to shape climate policy.

The end of the pastoralist mode of food production and land-use management in Tibet is in sight. As climate change becomes a core rationale for depopulating rural Tibet, displaced pastoralists – recast in official discourse as voluntary 'ecological migrants' – are now resettling in urban fringe settlements. Climate change, and the Chinese government's response, privileging grass and water over customary livelihoods, may soon succeed in closing huge areas to productive use, ending a strategy that has made Tibet habitable for thousands of years.

The mobility of Tibetan pastoralists, always moving on to avoid exhausting pastures, was in itself a response to an unpredictable climate. That mobility, long regarded with suspicion by China as primitive and uncivilized, has been forcibly restricted through successive strategies, first by compulsory collectivization, then by allocating land tenure to individual families while preventing customary seasonal rotations. With compulsory fencing and enforced stocking ratios further undermining the traditional pastoralist system, increasing blame has been heaped by the state on nomadic communities as the shrinking land allocations available to them have become insufficient to sustain their herds. This vicious circle is now approaching its final spiral. From beginning to end, nomadic lifestyles and the Chinese government's policies have been driven by differing approaches to climate change. Tibetan pastoralists are now being cleared from their land in the name of environmental conservation, overlooking centuries of accumulated skill and wisdom in managing the vast and challenging space of the Tibetan Plateau.

Tibet: Nomads caught between climate change and government 'conservation'

Vanuatu: Indigenous language loss and the multiplying effects of climate change

Anastasia Riehl

Members of a coastal community on their boat in front of an outcrop in Vanuatu. Photo supplied by Anastasia Riehl.

Rising from the deep waters of the South Pacific Ocean, an archipelago of erupting volcanos, bright blue inland marine holes, towering banyan forests and prolonged stretches of smooth sand beaches comprise the country of Vanuatu. These diverse landscapes, spread over 80 islands, have fostered a rich array of life – not only of plants and animals, but also of peoples and cultures. Dozens of distinct communities practising unique traditions and speaking different languages thrive throughout these islands.

The country's geography, which has gifted this diversity, is both its blessing and its curse; Vanuatu has the privilege of being the country with the most indigenous languages per capita, alongside the misfortune of being one of those most immediately at risk from climate change. These islands offer a window into one of the lesser-discussed threats of our changing climate: the threat to indigenous languages and global linguistic diversity.

Today the world is rich with languages – approximately 7,000 of them. But as the days pass, the numbers fall. Language scholars broadly agree that within the next 100 years, more than half of the world's languages will have gone extinct (meaning that no native speaker of a language remains). This decline has already begun, and news stories regularly mourn the passing of a 'last speaker'. There are many causes of this loss. Governments typically support national languages over regional languages in education and media. Persecuted groups face pressure to abandon minority and indigenous languages. Global conflicts lead to the splintering of linguistic communities during refugee crises. Technological advances in communication and transportation facilitate interaction between formerly distant communities. Globalization necessitates the use of large international languages for political and economic purposes. Now add to this list a new and exacerbating factor: climate change. As climate

> Today the world is rich with languages – **approximately 7,000** of them. But as the days pass, the numbers fall. Language scholars broadly agree that within the next 100 years, **more than half of the world's languages** will have gone extinct

change threatens the sustainability of indigenous communities throughout the globe, it also threatens their languages – languages that are already struggling to survive.

Climate change will ultimately affect all countries and peoples in the world. The most immediate and extreme effects, however, will be felt by tropical island states, which are particularly vulnerable to the rise of sea levels, warming ocean temperatures and increasingly destructive cyclones. Plans for relocating communities displaced by climate change are either under way or being discussed for the Maldives in the Indian Ocean and for low-lying coral atolls in the Pacific such as Kiribati, Tuvalu and the Marshall Islands. These areas of the world are disproportionately rich in indigenous languages, as each small island or nation is typically home to one or more distinct languages or dialects. As people are forced to leave their lands and relocate to other communities, they must adapt to new languages, and maintaining their own indigenous languages is a significant challenge.

Vanuatu is one of these states at the forefront of climate vulnerability. In 2015, the country was devastated by Cyclone Pam, a category 5 tropical cyclone cited as one of Vanuatu's worst environmental disasters of all time, which completely destroyed the infrastructure of many villages and severely affected the nation's economy. While environmental hazards such as cyclones and floods, as well as tectonic activity like earthquakes and volcanic eruptions, have long been part of life for the people of these islands, there is increasing evidence that climate change may be contributing to the intensity and frequency of such

events. The grave injustice is that Vanuatu, whose people live mostly in self-sustaining villages and produce very few fossil fuels, did not create this climate change disaster yet will be among its earliest and most deeply affected victims. In 2018, Vanuatu's Foreign Minister Ralph Regenvanu announced that the country would be the first to explore legal means to 'shift the costs of climate protection back onto the fossil fuel companies, the financial institutions and the governments that actively and knowingly created this existential threat to my country.'

This existential threat extends to the country's languages. Vanuatu is home to over 100 indigenous languages, from the 900 speakers of Aneityum at the southernmost tip to the 250 speakers of Hiu at the northernmost. With such a large number of languages and a total population of only 270,000 people, Vanuatu is believed to be the most linguistically diverse country on Earth. These languages have had the good fortune to thrive in a country that embraces, rather than suppresses, indigenous identities. The island state is rather unusual in its support of its languages: the government formally recognizes the indigenous languages in its charter and supports mother tongue language programming in elementary schools. These efforts reflect a more general movement to respect, celebrate and maintain indigenous cultural practices. But these efforts are in a battle against the myriad of stressors taking aim at the country's languages.

Vanuatu's languages exist in a linguistically complex environment. The country has three official languages: English, French and Bislama. The first two, left by colonial powers

Britain and France, who jointly governed the country until independence in 1980, remain the primary languages of education and business and are imperative for anyone seeking opportunities outside the country. The third official language, Bislama, is a creole based on grammatical structures from local Melanesian languages but with vocabulary primarily from English. It arose during the 1880s when Vanuatu's people were forced to work on plantations in Australia and Fiji. Bislama now serves as a lingua franca and is spoken by almost everyone as a second language and increasingly as a first language for those in the capital city, Port Vila, and those from linguistically mixed families.

Encouraging the use of the official languages, particularly Bislama, are developments in communication and transportation. A mobile phone network, launched just over 10 years ago, now connects islands that never had landline capabilities, and a new ring road on the main island of Efate greatly eases movement between communities previously accessible to one another

A flooded village in Vanuatu. Photo supplied by Anastasia Riehl.

only by boat or long treks on foot. (The road was just recently reopened after repairs following the destruction of Cyclone Pam.) While most would agree that these developments are positive for the country, they come at the cost of placing additional strain on its indigenous languages.

Now climate change is exacerbating these effects, threatening to destabilize the foundation that has bolstered Vanuatu's indigenous languages for centuries – traditional village life. Spread over dozens of islands, across disparate pieces of coastline, separated from one another by a wide river, a steep interior or the ocean waters, a number of relatively isolated indigenous communities have developed. These communities have thrived for centuries thanks to a climate that supports abundant resources – forests filled with fruit trees and edible plants, vast fish stocks and rich soils for subsistence farming. This sustainability has helped earn the country a 'world's happiest' ranking in international surveys of wellbeing. In these villages, without reliance on outside interactions, distinct indigenous languages and cultures have flourished. Now, however, as coastal areas become uninhabitable and weather changes adversely affect farming and fishing, some communities will be forced to relocate. This movement will bring different linguistic groups closer together in the fewer habitable areas and increase the number of people moving to Port Vila, environments that foster use of Bislama and decrease use of the indigenous languages.

Language loss may not seem as significant as the other losses Vanuatu and the world face in a changing climate, but it is far from solely a sentimental one. Languages are foundational to identity, the principal means for conveying a community's culture and heritage. This is why indigenous communities in North America, rebuilding their societies after decades of persecution, are prioritizing language revitalization alongside efforts to improve education and health care. Languages are also an invaluable source of information about the brain: loss of a language before it has been documented is a loss of scientific data needed to understand cognition, and, sadly, most endangered languages have yet to be studied or recorded. Finally, languages encode information about the natural world: the dozens of types of vines twisting into the trees on the Vanuatu island of Malakula, referred to by their thickness, rate of growth and distance from the ocean, have names in the local Na'ahai language but not in Bislama, and likely not in any other language.

Change is coming to the world's languages. Many will not survive the great shifts ahead, while others will persevere against the odds. For communities dedicated to preserving their languages, the right planning and resources will help them succeed. Unfortunately, climate change's multiplying effects shorten the timeframe and rob them of the necessary resources, making the challenge that much greater. Among the many critical reasons that humanity must fight to mitigate the looming climate crisis is the need to save the languages of Vanuatu and the linguistic diversity of the planet. ■

Europe

While it is sometimes framed in terms of future threats or distant disasters in other regions, the reality of climate change is already being felt in Europe. In the Arctic region, in particular, its impacts are reflected in rapidly melting glaciers and the accompanying destruction of indigenous cultures that for millennia have depended on these precious ecosystems for their survival.

For the thousands of reindeer herders in the northern regions of Russia and the Nordic countries, ice loss has disrupted traditional migration routes and exposed their animals to hunger, disease and population decline. Furthermore, as the changing environment has opened up larger swathes of indigenous territory to development, communities are now contending with encroachments on their land by companies and governments with mining, oil and other projects that endanger their way of life. So far, their calls for meaningful steps to prevent environmental collapse have gone unheeded.

The persistent inaction from European countries on climate change, then, is in part a continuation of the long-standing marginalization of indigenous peoples from political participation and decision-making. Yet climate change is also likely to take a heavy toll across Europe in other forms. Air pollution, for example, is now recognized as the cause of a major health crisis in Europe, responsible for half a million premature deaths every year. The risks, however, are distributed unevenly, with minorities and other disadvantaged groups among those most affected. For example, research has shown that in large European cities like London, the highest levels of pollution are typically in ethnically diverse neighbourhoods with significant minority populations. Climate change, besides being closely linked with air pollution and its causes, is also projected to intensify air pollution in Europe as a result of rising temperatures – and, in many areas, minorities will be the worst affected.

At the same time, climate change and environmental degradation elsewhere may be contributing to a shift in the demographic make-up of Europe. While the large-scale movement of migrants and asylum seekers from Africa, Asia and the Middle East into Europe in the last few years is often described in media and policy discussions as a 'flood' or 'wave', conjuring the imagery of natural disasters, the concept of 'climate refugees' remains contested. However, while persecution, conflict, poverty and the search for better opportunities remain the primary factors driving migration from these regions, there is evidence that environmental pressures may intersect with these forces to increase migration. Given the stated focus of European immigration policy to address the root causes of migration in sending countries, this is clearly an area that will need to be better understood in future to develop a humane and effective approach – grounded in evidence and respect for human rights – to immigration.

Bulgaria: The Roma community that got trapped in a coal pit

Vesselina Foteva

Smoke and vapor rise from chimney and cooling towers of the coal-fired thermal power plant 'Republika', in Pernik, Bulgaria. Alamy / *Johann Brandstatter*

Bulgaria's Roma population, one of the largest per capita in Europe, is among the country's most marginalized communities and Roma frequently experience unemployment, social exclusion and economic exploitation. Bulgaria also has one of the highest levels of air pollution, with elevated levels of fine particulate matter from burning coal and waste – a practice on which much of its electricity industry depends.

In 2017, Bulgaria became the first European country to lose a case in the European Court of Justice for its particularly poor air quality, and pollution continues to take a heavy toll on human health and the environment.

These two issues converge in the Bulgarian town of Pernik. Pernik is a town in western Bulgaria with a population of about 80,000 people, located 40 kilometres from the capital city of Sofia. According to official data, the Roma population in Pernik is around 3,500 people, but even the municipality of Pernik contests this figure: in reality, though the exact number is unknown, the community is much larger.

At the beginning of the last century, following the discovery of large deposits of brown coal in the area, the town became an industrial hub. Monumental slogans like 'Glory to the Labour of the Pitman' can be seen everywhere in town, and many in Pernik still proudly argue that Sofia was chosen as the capital city only because of its relative proximity to the natural riches of the 'Black Gold Town'. Today, though,

the splendour of this jewel of Bulgaria's mining industry shines no more. The tens of kilometres of tunnels, which cover roughly two-thirds of the area of the town, are all closed, and only one open-pit mine is still in operation.

Unofficially, though, the mining goes on. In the last decade, there have been regular reports of illegal coal mining – and those typically suspected and frequently referred to in local media as 'moles' are Roma. What is usually left out of this analysis, however, is the poverty and exploitation that has driven a small number of community members to engage in this dangerous practice, and the fact that those worst affected are overwhelmingly Roma.

Roma and illegal mining

'Horror houses: Illegal mining destroys houses in Pernik

16 arrested for illegal coal mining near Pernik

Illegal coal mining leads to a landslide in Rudnichar in Pernik'

Bulgaria: The Roma community that got trapped in a coal pit

This is how the media reports on the increasing prevalence of illegal coal mining in old and abandoned mines near Pernik. Those arrested are usually Roma or sometimes former coal miners looking for some additional income.

'Near Ursata natural park is located the now closed mine owned by the Bulgarian–Belgian company Recoal, which is still operating, but illegally. The local institutions were turning a blind eye, so that there would be some livelihood for the minorities', says Genadi Kondarev, coordinator for Social Funding for Sustainable Development with the non-governmental organization (NGO) For the Earth. He has been fighting against climate change and illegal coal mining for years.

Ursata natural park is a forest that was supposed to separate Pernik from the open-pit mine just outside the town. In 2005, however, Recoal won a concession and started mining right in the centre of the forest. In 2015, when the contract ended, Recoal failed to fulfil its obligation to re-forest what it had destroyed. The inhabitants of the mostly Roma settlement nearby, known as Rudnichar, are still feeling the after-effects of this.

'There are 300 unsecured shafts, horizontal galleries and excavations deeper than 20 metres,' says Kondarev. 'They are being used even today by people, including young children, to mine coal.' At first the mining was for personal use only, but over time it became more organized and the coal is now being sold on the black market for as little as a tenth of its market value. And on the mining went, until eventually three houses in the settlement collapsed.

And though the 'moles' themselves live in Rudnichar, Kondarev reports that 'it is hard to talk with them' as many now fear losing their income and prosecution for their activities.

A community sickened by mining

The Roma community in Rudnichar prefers not to talk about the illegal mining, but a short walk through the unpaved streets of the neighbourhood shows that almost every house has some coal near the front door and there are lots of small warehouses. Nobody hides the issues created by the now closed mine of Recoal.

The walls of Maria's house (the names of all Roma community members have been changed) are cracked because of the landslides, but she has not left it. 'Everyone does what they can in order to get some food on the table here. Sixty years I've lived here, practically since I was born. It was really nice here. Now it's decaying. They cut down the forest. Dug, dug, the rich people, got the coal, took the money, and left. It's scary when you think about it.' She used to let her children play in the forest, but now doesn't allow her grandchildren even close to it. 'How can I let them go there? It's a swamp, a hole, a wasteland!'

'The Belgian guy was a troublemaker!' adds her neighbour, Alexander. 'His baggers dug here, then left it in ruins. I let the children play only in front of the door, you can't let them go farther!' But when asked about the local 'moles', he says that he does not know any and walks on.

Another resident talks more openly. 'In the night, they use lights to dig. The police tried really hard to stop this, but failed. It's not a joke at all – 13 people got buried in the ground. They mine to sell, not for personal use. This is fast money, but who knows – one night you go back home, but the next you might be left underground.'

Kondarev has been reporting on the issue for years. The diggers don't understand how they influence their own communities, but he thinks that the Roma people are being exploited. So far, unofficial estimates suggest that there may have been more than a dozen deaths as a result of accidents from illegal mining, but 'there is not even any official data on that'. Recoal's failure to re-forest the area has enabled continued mining and other illegal activities, such as logging, that in turn have resulted in landslides, flooding and adverse effects on the health of the inhabitants themselves. 'The big money players use the people. For them, the people, they don't mean anything, their life is worthless. They just send them, give them a few dimes for every sack of coal, and whoever goes out of the ground is out. Whoever doesn't – doesn't.'

The big picture

The illegal coal mining near Pernik turns out to be part of a bigger problem – one that, while attracting criticism from a variety of health and environmental organizations, appears largely to be accepted by Bulgaria's government and industry.

Coal fuels an industry that has been widely accepted as harmful to the environment and a major contributor not only to air pollution, but also to climate change. In Bulgaria there are eight coal-fuelled power plants currently in operation, including the Republika power plant in Pernik, and coal burning – responsible for a third of the country's CO_2 emissions – generates more than 40 per cent of the nation's electricity.

Coal is largely responsible for the extraordinarily high levels of fine particulate matter in Bulgaria, a major cause of respiratory diseases with deadly implications. The World Health Organization (WHO) has cautioned that the country has the third highest mortality caused by air pollution in the world, after only North Korea and Bosnia and Herzegovina, and has called for immediate measures from the Bulgarian government.

In addition, the European Environment Agency reported in 2013 that four of

In Bulgaria there are **eight coal-fuelled power plant**s currently in operation, including the Republika power plant in Pernik, and coal burning – responsible **for a third of the country's CO_2 emissions** – generates more than 40 per cent per cent of the nation's electricity.

Bulgaria: The Roma community that got trapped in a coal pit

the five most air-polluted European cities were located in Bulgaria, with Pernik topping the list – a situation reflected in research by advocacy groups such as the 'Pernik Breathes' Association. 'We have mobile measuring stations which we have placed in our homes to examine the air quality before we open the windows,' says Ivaylo Velinov, a member of the association. 'With the start of the winter the air gets unbreathable.'

Although Bulgaria is one of the many countries that adopted the Paris Agreement, business continues as usual in the municipality of Pernik. Climate change activists warn that the municipality has received four investment proposals to support the burning of more than a hundred different types of waste to generate electricity. If implemented, this would likely worsen the air significantly. And, at a broader level, while a growing number of countries proudly declare their deadlines for the cessation of coal mining and

its use for energy production, Bulgaria has demonstrated no intention of shifting to a cleaner energy source. This is reflected in the statement of the President of Bulgaria, Rumen Radev, at the UN Climate Change Conference in Katowice, Poland in December 2018. 'We strongly disagree with the unnecessarily high requirements for the reduction of greenhouse gas emissions,' he said then. 'We must keep coal mines in Bulgaria because this means keeping jobs and guaranteeing security.'

Ignoring the consequences of climate change by focusing on the economic security of the community – despite the fact that the WHO estimates the cost of air pollution to Bulgaria from premature deaths at 29.5 per cent of its national GDP – is a well-proven tool for shifting the topic, skilfully used by the local authorities as well. They tolerate the thriving black market for coal by imposing only nominal control over the restoration of the many abandoned mines. In addition, those residents involved in illegal mining are rarely sanctioned effectively for their actions, or offered the opportunity to engage in alternative livelihoods. Instead, the illegally mined coal is left to infiltrate seamlessly into the local economy. What is needed instead is a transformative strategy, founded on climate justice, to navigate the country towards a greener and more equitable future. This would bring significant benefits to all Bulgarians and prevent many of the more than 15,000 premature deaths that currently occur in the country every year as a result of air pollution. Beyond that, however, there needs to be greater recognition of the poverty and discrimination that has locked marginalized communities such as Rudnichar's Roma in a vicious

The European Environment Agency reported in 2013 that **four of the five most air-polluted** European cities were located in Bulgaria, with Pernik topping the list...

The cracked house belonging to Maria in the neighbourhood of Rudnichar in Pernik, Bulgaria. Photo supplied by Vesselina Foteva.

cycle of contamination, exploitation and ill health. While stronger regulations would go a long way to protecting them from the worst effects of the illegal mining, authorities also need to invest in providing residents with better opportunities elsewhere. Until the underlying barriers separating Roma communities from other Bulgarians are addressed, it is likely they will continue to find themselves on the frontline of the country's ongoing environmental crisis.

All names of members of the Roma community have been changed at their request. Contacts with the local Roma community were established with the kind support of the 'PULSE' Foundation.

Finland: 'Instability and abnormality are the new normal. Weather can change in an instant.'

A portrait of Klemetti Näkkäläjärvi, a Sámi researcher and activist in Finland. Photo supplied by Oula-Antti Labba

Klemetti Näkkäläjärvi, a Sámi researcher and member of
the Galggojávri Sámi reindeer-herding community, has worked
for years on the impact of climate change on the Sámi people.
Here he explains to Oula-Antti Labba how climate change
is transforming their way of life, with traditional livelihoods
and local species increasingly under threat.

Climate change, lifestyle change and the new exploitation of Arctic resources create clear threats to the Sámi and Sámi culture. The first signs of a changed climate were observed in the 1960s on the basis of the findings of Sámi reindeer owners. The changes observed relate to seasons, temperature, extreme conditions, vegetation, fauna, wind, snow and reindeer life. The most significant changes, however, concern uncertainty – forecasting conditions is difficult and the variability between years has increased significantly, making it challenging to work with the reindeer and plan ahead.

In different areas, the effects will be different. Changes are already visible in vegetation; the most significant change that has been observed by reindeer herders is the rise of the tree line on the north slopes and also in the fells. The trees are also growing faster and growing back more quickly after forest fires, which makes it difficult for both reindeer and herders to move across forest pastures. The *palsas* (a frost heave or mound with a core of ice) have started to melt. In my own childhood village, Nunnas still had *palsas* in the 1980s – nowadays there are only the usual swamps. Changes in rainfall and vegetation make herding work difficult, and the combination of wind with rain especially increases the risk of erosion. The greening of the Sámi land accelerates climate change and affects the local climate, because the snow melts faster in wooded and scrubland areas. It can easily be detected in the spring, with snow melting around the trees faster.

Last year was an example of how the climate has changed. The dry and hot summer of 2018 added heat stress to the reindeer; the calf markings could not be held in all areas because the reindeer died in enclosures. In Sweden, record-breaking forest fires destroyed the reindeer pastures across a wide area, shrinking pastures for a long time. The early winter was also exceptional – warm and snowless. Usually, snowmobiles would have been in use in Sápmi in the second week of November at the latest, but they were not needed until December.

Finland: 'Instability and abnormality are the new normal. Weather can change in an instant.'

Reindeer separation by Sámi herders in Inari, Lapland, Finland. Alamy / *Jorge Duarte Estevao*

Reindeer-herding as a livelihood can adapt to climate change with the help of additional feeding and technology, but reindeer-herding as a Sámi cultural livelihood is greatly endangered in Finland. Changes in traditional livelihoods directly affect the Sámi identity and the vitality of the their culture. In addition to the Sámi languages, they are a link to the early history of Sámi culture. Climate change, on the other hand, may accelerate the trend of Sámi people moving out of their native region, but at the same time increase the number of the majority population moving in.

If this trend accelerates, the Sámi are in danger of becoming a linguistic minority. Opportunities to maintain the Sámi culture in urban areas are limited. It means adaptation, cultural change, loss, threats and problems – both physical and mental. In the worst case scenario, it will contribute to accelerating the integration of the Sámi into the mainstream culture. Researchers have reported that the changed circumstances have brought the Sámi stress and concern about the future of their own culture and way of life.

The most concrete health impact of climate change is the increase in accidents. My informants have reported a number of near-miss situations that have been caused by the fact that the ice did not withstand movement, as temperature fluctuations and large amounts of snow had weakened its carrying capacity, and the conditions were no longer what the reindeer were accustomed to. The survival strategy is to work and travel in groups, because it is difficult to get help quickly and a large part of the area is outside the mobile network.

'The palsas (a frost heave or mound with a core of ice) have started to melt. In my own childhood village, Nunnas still had palsas in the 1980s – nowadays there are only the usual swamps. Changes in rainfall and vegetation make herding work difficult.'

There have been changes in species. Some alien species have come to Sámi under the influence of human activity – for example, raccoon dogs have been found in Kautokeino and roe deer are also found in Enontekiö. The reason is partly climate change, but above all human feeding. Our most important game species, the snow grouse, has suffered from a warming climate and is disappearing from its current territories in the central parts of the Arctic countries. Forestry and foxes are also contributing to its disappearance. Perhaps the most decisive thing to do is to consider how the reindeer can survive climate change itself. The reindeer are going hungry, and the warming conditions can be fatal for the Arctic animal.

By the end of the century, the climate in the Sámi region will be similar to the climate in southern Finland. Seasons have changed, but the warming climate brings new challenges – infrastructure, mining and industrial projects, as well as the environmental risks of the emerging Arctic sea route. In Finland, for example, there are ongoing discussions about the possibilities and boundary conditions for the implementation of the Arctic railway. It would not even be possible to talk about the Arctic railway plans without climate change.

We know less about the future effects of climate change than we should. There are a lot of causal relationships and things we don't yet understand.

Our region is so networked with global processes that our own actions have limited potential. It is generally said that what happens in the Arctic and with the climate does not stay in the Arctic. It could also be said that what happens in industrialized countries does not stay there, but comes directly or indirectly to the Sámi land – although then in the form of fine particles.

Climate change affects everyone and everything, from our brains all the way to micro-organisms. In human life, however, the changes are progressing quite slowly and one can adapt to them, but the question is how to maintain a culturally significant life and cultural richness also in the changing climate. Climate change is happening now and will be passed on to future generations. From the point of view of Sámi culture, the effects of climate change are intergenerational – the solutions and adaptations by this generation will be passed on to future generations as an inheritance, through changed business models, know-how, language and values and ideals.

Finland: 'Instability and abnormality are the new normal. Weather can change in an instant.'

Poland: The role of environmental factors in shaping migration from Maghreb countries to Europe

Karolina Sobczak-Szelc

16-year old Zahra Ennaji carries a jug of water across the sand towards her family's nomadic compound in the Sahara Desert near the southern village of Mhamid, Morocco. Panos / *Giacomo Pirozzi*

Algeria, Morocco and Tunisia have a long history of migration to Europe. The destinations have changed over time: while France, Belgium and the Netherlands were major targets at first, later North Mediterranean countries such as Spain, Italy or Greece have been favoured, and now, though still very low in numbers, more and more migrants choose Central and Eastern European countries as their destination, including Poland.

Though these migratory movements used to be explained in largely economic or social terms, driven by labour force needs in destination countries, family reunification, or the inequalities between the developed North and still developing South, there is growing recognition that other factors may also be involved. Indeed, although economic forces continue to be the most important driver of movement between North Africa and Europe, many studies suggest that environmental factors may also be playing a role in the decision of some to migrate.

This is illustrated by the situation of inhabitants of the villages in the High Atlas Mountains, whose fields, contained by steep valley slopes, are inundated and covered with sand and stones by flash floods every year. In a very different context, oasis communities on the edge of the Sahara also struggle with environmental pressures as crops are dependent on erratic rainfall, limited groundwater supplies or water delivered from a reservoir hundreds of kilometres away. In many cases, climate change impacts may exacerbate existing social or economic issues. In desert areas of Tunisia, for example, where local agriculture relies on underground water reserves, access to them is limited by insufficient investments in infrastructure and further jeopardized by degradation of these precious water supplies. Other man-made changes, such as river diversion, dam construction and uncontrolled drilling, are also factors contributing to environmental scarcity and stress, but are again exacerbated by an increasingly extreme and unpredictable climate.

These are some of the challenges of everyday life in the arid and semi-arid regions of North Africa, and they may push some inhabitants to look for alternative sources of income to traditional agriculture. In these cases, migration may be the only feasible option. Mohamed,* an inhabitant of Mhamid in southern Morocco, where lack of water, degradation of vegetation and the spread of dunes have made traditional livelihoods increasingly difficult, has two sons who have both left the region to look for work elsewhere.

As he explains:

"You can't work any more in agriculture due to climate change. One year is good and then you have five or ten years of drought. That's why my sons won't stay here. They decided that they won't stay here because, if it is good here for two years, it is good, but then there is drought and you have no work.'

Although the decision to migrate is complex and is often closely tied to social, economic and cultural considerations, such as the search for employment and networks with migrant communities elsewhere, research points to the significant role that environmental factors can play. It should be noted that within the Maghreb region, much of this migration takes place within countries, as members of rural communities relocate to larger cities to work in tourism, construction or other sectors. Given the restrictive policies in place across Europe and the significant costs associated with travel to Europe, whether through official channels or by other means, for most North Africans the possibility of reaching Europe remains remote.

Nevertheless, despite the increasing hostility of many European states to immigration, there is a long history of migration between certain countries, such as Tunisia and France, and migration continues to provide some North African nationals with the opportunity to alleviate shortfalls in agriculture and other sectors in their home countries by looking for work in Europe. Those who manage to reach Europe have a chance to earn enough money to support their relatives back home – thus providing not only the migrant but also his or her extended

family with a coping strategy. In the current context, however, most are forced to attempt the journey to Europe through clandestine means, and only a minority of those who try succeed in doing so. And for those family members left behind, often struggling with economic and environmental challenges, the situation can be just as desperate.

Nationals of Maghreb countries make up a large proportion of both documented and undocumented migrants in the European Union (EU). According to EUROSTAT data, for example, in 2017 the largest group of new citizens in the EU member states were citizens of Morocco – 67,900, corresponding to 8.2 per cent of all citizenships granted. Meanwhile, in terms of irregular border crossings into the EU, FRONTEX figures show that Morocco, Algeria and Tunisia are among the top 10 sending countries. And although, in comparison to Western Europe, the number of migrants from Maghreb countries in Poland is still very low, there has nevertheless been a substantial rise in the number of citizens of those countries, whether arriving through official channels with a residence permit or trying to enter Poland clandestinely.

This is despite evidence of increasing hostility towards Muslims, migrants and refugees in Polish society, encouraged by divisive and inflammatory rhetoric in some mainstream media. But while migration itself has become an increasingly politicized issue – in particular, populist parties have managed to exploit xenophobic sentiments to boost their electoral share – there is still relatively little discussion of the different factors, including climate change and environmental stress, that may be driving this movement. With better information and more open discussion, it is possible that some of the stigma and misunderstandings faced by migrant communities in Europe might be reduced.

Ali, an Amazigh (or Berber) migrant from the Upper Dades Valley in Morocco, now living in Poland, emphasizes the dilemmas that many younger Moroccans feel when they decide to migrate. 'It's not that they don't want to stay,' Ali says. 'They need to earn. They need to earn to survive. That's why, if they stay there, they cannot make it.' He is quick to identify environmental instability as a major factor in this.

'You are at risk. Why? It is a mountainous area, each year the river swells over. More or less, the area is flooded. And the commodities get spoiled, wasted. So always they are at risk. Because these people, they rely on natural resources.'

The situation in the Dades Valley has deteriorated in large part due to the degradation of the local environment, as reduced vegetation cover has reduced water retention capacity in the area and so made it more vulnerable to flooding.

Today, people from those areas within the Maghreb that are most dependent on agriculture, and where young people have few or no prospects, face most pressure to migrate. The desperation of some is sufficiently strong that they are willing, despite Europe's increasingly restrictive migration policy, to attempt the dangerous crossing of the Mediterranean in makeshift boats – a journey that frequently proves deadly, as was the case in November 2018 when a small boat full of migrants travelling towards the Canary Islands capsized near the coast of Tiznit province in Morocco. Only three people, all with Moroccan nationality, managed to reach the shore and alert the authorities. The other 22 migrants went missing in the waters off Morocco's Atlantic coast.

The links between climate change, environmental stress and migration to Europe in the Maghreb remain uncertain, and the variety of social and economic forces pushing thousands of Moroccans to leave their country are sufficiently complex that it is difficult to attribute the decision to migrate to climate change alone. Nevertheless, as understanding of this difficult issue improves, it may be the case that migration to Europe is framed not only as a coping strategy for unemployment and lack of opportunities, but also as an adaptive response to a changing climate.

In 2017 the largest group of new citizens in the EU member states were citizens of Morocco – **67,900**, corresponding to **8.2 per cent** of all citizenships granted. Meanwhile, in terms of irregular border crossings into the EU, FRONTEX figures show that Morocco, Algeria and Tunisia are among **the top 10 sending countries.**

Russia: A way of life under threat for Nenets as oil drilling and ice melt take their toll

Charlotte Graham

A Nenets woman herding reindeers in the Western Siberian Yamal Peninsula, Russia.
Alamy / *Steve Morgan*

Nenets are an indigenous Siberian people, whose traditional economy has long been rooted in nomadic reindeer-herding, fishing and hunting. The majority inhabit the Yamal Peninsula – meaning 'edge of the world' in the Nenets language. Though the Nenets live on the fringes of industrialized society, they are among the first populations to face the consequences of a changing climate.

Nenets came under Russian influence from the sixteenth century onwards. Under Soviet rule they were forcibly collectivized and their shamanist religion was attacked. A number of Nenets rebellions took place from the 1930s, but the community was largely sedentarized in the 1950s, and the region later saw a large influx of Slavic settlers employed in industry.

In 1990s the Russian energy company Gazprom initiated preparations for one of its biggest oil projects, the Yamal Megaproject, aimed at exploiting the peninsula's gas reserves. This process soon led to large-scale destruction of plant cover and vegetation in the Yamal Peninsula, beginning a long period of environmental deterioration. In 2012, the first gas supplies were produced from the vast Bovanenkovo reserve, and billions of cubic metres of gas are now piped to Western Europe. As a result of this exploitation, many indigenous inhabitants have had to leave the Yamal Peninsula for fear of being forced to live in permanent settlements.

Today, the main problems confronting the Nenets are ecological damage deriving from exploitation of the Yamal region's natural gas deposits, unemployment and alcoholism. Their nomadic lifestyle is now threatened as their migration routes have been disrupted by mining infrastructure, pollution and the effects of climate change. As a result, many young Nenets are forced to migrate to cities, where they frequently struggle to integrate and face a range of social problems.

As with other indigenous communities in the Russian Federation that depend on reindeer-herding for their cultures and livelihoods, a further key threat to the Nenets' future is climate change. Warmer summers bring higher and denser shrub growth across the tundra, making it more difficult to gather and move reindeer herds. Rapid shifts in temperature can cause freezing rain, which, in turn, causes the lichen that reindeer depend on to be covered by a thick and often impenetrable layer of ice, with many dying as a result.

Russia: A way of life under threat for Nenets as oil drilling and ice melt take their toll

And the untimely melting of lake and river ice can make it difficult for Nenets to follow their reindeer's traditional migration patterns. Indeed, certain parts of the permafrost that Nenets and their reindeer need to cross have ceased to exist in some places, and are only accessible in colder months elsewhere. Though Nenets also rely on hunting and fishing, reindeer herds are the sole livelihood of many, so a negative impact on this one species can be destructive for the entire community. Moreover, reindeer-herding is central to Nenets' culture and traditions. Changing migration paths and scarcer pastures also mean that families have less access to medical services as they are forced to camp further from towns. Nenets can adapt by continuing to roam widely in search of pastures: the issue is whether mining and natural gas extraction will hamper their access to the necessary range of habitats. Ever-expanding gas and oil industries encroach on reindeer pasture territory, and so regions on the Yamal Peninsula (where the nomadic Nenets live and move around) are overgrazed. In addition, the new pipelines and other industrial infrastructure are creating further obstacles to traditional migration routes.

Empty oil barrels discarded on Nenets traditional land in the Western Siberian Yamal Peninsula, Russia. Alamy / *Steve Morgan*

Sadly, these impacts look likely to intensify in the coming years as the region continues to be targeted for development and fossil fuel extraction. The Yamal Peninsula holds more than one-fifth of Russia's natural gas reserves, roughly as much as the entire reserves of the United States. These natural gas fields are situated along major herding routes, and there is currently a proposed pipeline to connect hubs at Bovanenkovo (already the largest gas field in Yamal, which herds must cross to reach summer pastures) and Payuta with oil and gas terminals. Proposed railways also cut straight through traditional Nenets routes. A new gas field called Kruzenshternskoye is to be constructed in the next few years on the Kara Sea coast, which will destroy prime areas of pasture, meaning even less grazing access for already weakened reindeer.

Many prominent activists from the Nenets community, specifically the Forest Nenets, have spoken publicly about the environmental challenges facing their community. Yuri Vella, for example, a prominent poet, environmentalist and social activist, was a former reindeer herder in the tundra of the Agan River who later organized protests on behalf of the Nenets people in Yamal, Varagansk, to raise awareness on the encroachment of gas and oil industries on their traditional territories. Vella also wrote in the Forest Nenets language, a significant move in an era in which most Nenets were encouraged to adopt Russian and discard their native language.

In the face of these changes, the Nenets people continue to be flexible and adaptive: they regularly cross pipelines and railroads and other Russian operations to follow their traditional migration routes, but climate change and the deteriorating local environment nevertheless pose an existential threat to every aspect of their lives. With the depletion of the natural resources on which they depend, an entire way of life goes too. Some Nenets have already responded to these changes by leaving their nomadic communities and assimilating in urban communities, though many reportedly struggle with high levels of alcoholism, unemployment and mental health issues as a result.

This profile is an edited version of the community profile featured in the Russian Federation country entry of MRG's World Directory of Minorities and Indigenous Peoples. ▉

Russia: A way of life under threat for Nenets as oil drilling and ice melt take their toll

A Nenets woman chops wood outside her 'choom' in temperatures of -40 Celsius in Naryan-Mar, Russia. Panos / *Justin Jin*

Middle East and North Africa

Across the Middle East and North Africa, protracted dry spells, heatwaves and drought have long posed challenges to communities in the region. However, these extremes are already intensifying as a result of climate change, and in the future could result in increasing food insecurity, water shortages and crop failure.

For both settled farming communities and the dwindling numbers of pastoralists who depend on land and water to graze their herds, the scarcity of these resources has placed their traditional way of life under strain – and in some cases, brought the two populations into conflict. Many formerly nomadic populations in countries such as Morocco, however, have been forced to abandon their lifestyle altogether as climate change, deforestation and other pressures have destroyed the livelihoods that once sustained them.

Many countries already contending with civil conflict and violence, such as Iraq and Yemen, now face the added challenge of responding to the pressures of a changing climate and the accompanying social disruption this will likely create. While some studies have suggested a direct causal link between climate change and the emergence of ethno-religious conflict, including in Syria, the concept of so-called 'climate wars' in the region is strongly contested by others who point instead to the importance of poor governance, communal tensions and other factors in driving conflict. Nevertheless, while the connections are far from simple and any analysis of climate change impacts in the region needs to be situated in the wider political, social and economic context of each country, it is likely that further competition and resource scarcity in future will disproportionately affect marginalized minorities and indigenous peoples.

This is illustrated by the situation of communities such as Iraq's Marsh Arabs, long dependent on their local environment for their survival and still recovering from years of persecution under Saddam Hussein, who now find their existing poverty and exclusion deepened by the impacts of climate change in their territory. It is also clear that any effective response to climate change in the region will also require meaningful collaboration between different groups and interests – a scenario that can only be realized through transparent governance structures as well as proper respect by all sides for the region's diversity. The importance of an inclusive framework grounded in human rights for all, particularly minorities and indigenous peoples, is therefore a prerequisite for any successful adaptation strategies.

Iraq: 'Women are the backbone of the Marsh Arab community – as the effects of climate change are becoming more visible, it is becoming clearer that women are the first to suffer.'

Ali Khadr

A female Marsh Arab collecting reeds in the historic Marshes of southern Iraq, January 2018.
Ali Khadr

The Marsh Arabs, sometimes referred to as Ma'dan ('the dweller in the plains'), are inhabitants of the Tigris and Euphrates marshlands in the south and east of Iraq. Comprising different tribes, the Marsh Arabs have developed a unique culture that is firmly rooted in the aquatic environment of the marshes, a way of life that has been cultivated for thousands of years.

The Marsh Arabs of Iraq have long suffered from state marginalization, discrimination and violence, but they now face a new adversary – climate change. While water scarcity as a result of climate change is projected to be an acute challenge across the Middle East in the years to come, Iraq is especially vulnerable within the region. The southern marshlands of Iraq have already suffered significantly from shifting weather patterns and prolonged droughts, as well as man-made environmental changes. Soon, the numerous benefits that the marshes provide to their inhabitants may be lost – and with them, much of the distinctive Marsh Arab culture.

A history of environmental impact

The marshes of Iraq were once the largest wetlands in the Middle East and western Eurasia. In the 1970s, the marshes covered between 15,000 and 20,000 square kilometres of water surface and vegetation, comprising 17 per cent of the country's surface area. During the 1980s and 1990s, however, Saddam Hussein subjected the marshes and their inhabitants to large-scale targeted destruction. The Marsh Arabs were accused of treachery against the regime, and as punishment much of the marshes were drained. A dam was built along the Euphrates River, south of Nasiriya, and Earth barriers were used to block the tributaries of the Tigris River that fed the marshes. Simultaneously, the waters were poisoned, and economic blockades were placed upon a population already suffering from the consequences of American sanctions.

As a result, in the space of just a few years, an ancient culture was on the verge of annihilation: in one month alone, between December 1991 and January 1992, more than 70 villages were destroyed and over 50,000 inhabitants uprooted from their homes. Those who stayed faced

Mother and
children rushing
to seek shelter
from the storm,
Chibayish
Marshes, Iraq,
January 2018.

Ali Khadr

starvation and killings. A once thriving
community of almost half a million
in the 1950s dwindled to as little
as 20,000 by the end of Hussein's
rule. While some of the Marsh Arabs
sought refuge in neighbouring towns
and cities, many of them were forced
to flee to refugee camps in Iran.

Many of the Marsh Arab communities
that fled during the Saddam regime
returned to their homeland in 2003.
This was a remarkable period of
restoration as the marshes were
brought back to life, with large swathes
of the drained areas inundated once
again. Yet increasing water scarcity is
now threatening to undo much of this
progress. This challenge was brought
into sharp relief in the summer of 2018,
when Iraq suffered its worst water

shortage crisis in 80 years. This is in
part due to dam construction projects
in neighbouring countries, such as
Turkey's Southeastern Anatolian Project,
Syria's Tabqa dam and Iran's Karkheh
River dam, that have greatly reduced the
country's water supply. Mismanagement
of water resources within Iraq itself, as
well as other governance challenges,
have also played a major part in the
scarcity now afflicting the marshes.

Nevertheless, intersecting with these
issues are the effects of climate
change, with a recent report by the
Expert Working Group on Climate-
related Security Risks highlighting
'prolonged heatwaves, erratic
precipitation, higher than average
temperatures and increased disaster
intensity' as some of the most pressing

impacts now being felt in Iraq. Hotter spells and extended periods of drought have also led to a drop in water levels while at the same time salinity has risen to unhealthy levels. With temperatures currently reaching more than 40°C during the summer and predicted to rise by an average of 2°C by 2050, these effects are likely only to intensify in future.

Living with climate change in the marshlands

Combined with the added environmental stresses of poor water management and dam construction, climate change will affect the lives of Iraq's Marsh Arabs in myriad ways. This is illustrated, to some extent, by the water crisis of 2018 and its impact on local agriculture, with livestock devastated in some areas of southern Iraq and hundreds of farming families reportedly forced to leave their homes in search of better irrigated land elsewhere. As many communities are largely dependent on agriculture for their livelihood, rising temperatures, drought and more frequent sand storms could increase the risk of displacement and migration. According to the Director of Antiquities and Heritage in Basra, Qahtan Al Abeed, the extent of the damage caused by fluctuating water levels in the marshes has driven many Marsh Arabs to leave their villages and head to the inner cities to make a living, returning only seasonally, depending on water levels.

Health is another area where climate change is projected to take a heavy toll. As reed production declines, and with it an important natural buffer for the hot winds that blow through the marshes, hotter temperatures and dust clouds from the desiccated marsh beds will have serious impacts on the Marsh Arab population. These include respiratory sicknesses, cancer and higher levels of infant mortality.

And, as elsewhere, women are likely to be particularly affected by these changes in the environment. Within the Marsh Arab community, women once played a very active role: while the men went out to fish, the women would gather reeds, herd water buffalo and other livestock, produce milk, cheese and yoghurt, make handicrafts such as rugs, scarfs and hand fans, look after the home and, at the end of the day, sell the fruits of their labour at the local market. 'Women,' says Al Abeed, 'are the backbone of the Marsh Arab community. As the effects of climate change are becoming more visible, it is becoming clearer that the women within the marshlands are the first to suffer.' The disappearance of

A once thriving community of almost **half a million in the 1950s** dwindled to as little as **20,000** by the end of Hussein's rule.

fresh water, reeds and other natural resources has severely constrained the role of women in their society and reports suggest that, as a result, they are no longer passing traditional knowledge to the younger generations.

Looking ahead

Iraq's ability to alleviate the impacts of climate change by modernizing water infrastructure and the agricultural sector have been debilitated by poor governance, corruption, war and the legacy of Saddam Hussein's decades-long rule. If left neglected, the combination of climate change impacts, decreased water flow from Iraq's neighbouring countries and poor infrastructure will create a catastrophe for the livelihoods and water security of hundreds of thousands of Iraqis, particularly the Marsh Arabs. According to Al Abeed, unexpected heavy rainfall over the wet season in 2019 resulted in the highest water levels the marshes have witnessed since 1975, indicating the drastic changes in weather patterns producing both droughts and floods.

With this in mind, the government has set up a working committee, headed by the Ministry of Water and joined by the Ministries of Culture, Environment, Oil, Agriculture and Education, tasked with ensuring the sustainable management of the marshes and the promotion of tourism in Iraq's marshlands to inject much needed cash flow into the local economy. The preservation of Marsh Arab livelihoods, culture and heritage is now heavily dependent on the success of the committee's initiatives. While the future remains uncertain, what is clear is that any lasting solution must be firmly rooted in a rights-based strategy to tackle climate change, addressing not only the changes in the local ecosystem but also their specific impacts on the Marsh Arab community themselves.

In one month alone, between December 1991 and January 1992, more than **70 villages were destroyed** and **over 50,000 inhabitants uprooted** from their homes.

Morocco: Rising tensions between nomadic pastoralists and sedentary communities over land and water

Nourredine Bessadi

In recent years, nomadic pastoralists in Souss, southern Morocco, have been coming into increased conflict with settled communities there. Water and land are at the heart of the conflict.

Although the overall number of remaining nomads has decreased significantly, with official estimates suggesting a decline from around 68,500 in 2004 to 25,300 in 2014, at the same time more and more nomads have been moving north, particularly to the Souss region, in search of land. These groups now stay longer, sometimes settling on the agricultural land of the predominantly Amazigh communities there – a situation that has led to at times deadly confrontations, especially as some groups of nomads are reportedly armed. With Amazigh struggling to protect their ancestral lands from encroachment on the one hand, and an impoverished nomadic population with little support from the Moroccan government to handle water shortages or lack of access to grazing on the other, there are challenges for both settled populations and pastoralists alike.

For Abdesslam, a Soussi based in Casablanca, 'what has led to the recent violent clashes in the Souss region is the strong presence of nomads attracted by the fertile land to graze their animals, but also to sell certain agricultural products they would steal.' The inhabitants of Souss call this 'wild pastoralism'. He adds that 'the Drâa River, the main source of water in the region, has suffered since the war [with Polisario Front] in the Sahara. The rain became more sporadic and temperatures got hotter.'

These pressures have already contributed to the erosion of traditional nomadic communities, with many families forced to relocate to urban areas as a means of survival. At the same time, for those who remain, relations with sedentary communities have become increasingly strained.

While for decades nomadic groups would settle in the Souss region, this was generally at well-defined periods in the seasonal migration cycle and largely confined to specific grazing areas. As water and pastures have become more scarce, however, access to land has become a source of confrontation between sedentary and nomadic populations.

With rising temperatures, reduced rainfall and longer spells of drought predicted as a result of climate change, these conflicts could intensify in future. With this in mind, in April 2018 a draft decree on the creation, development and management of pastoral areas was approved by the Government Council in Morocco. This project is part of the implementation of the provisions of law 113.13, relating to transhumance and the governance of pastoral areas. Officially, this project aims to create a framework for the management and development of pastoral areas to ensure their security and sustainability.

However, some residents of Souss consider this law to be a simple extension of discriminatory laws that date back to the colonial era and an inadequate response to the urgent need to manage the conflict between local residents and nomadic groups. This is sharpened by the sense that Moroccan authorities are themselves seen as violating the indigenous land rights of Amazigh in the region through overgrazing, mine development and the spread of wild boar for foreign game hunts, without meaningful consultation with the communities in question.

Indeed, in the eyes of many Amazigh, in the decades since independence Morocco has continued the environmental despoliation carried out under French colonial rule, when laws were passed to 'legalize' the dispossession of tribal territory and resources by the state. All this has accentuated their feelings of marginalization and stoked widespread protests throughout the latter part of 2018 against the Moroccan government. In response, the Akal Coordination Group, an alliance of local NGOs focusing on land rights, has called for the abolition of 'dahirs, laws and colonial decrees expropriating the indigenous peoples from their lands', as well as a more participatory approach to decision-making in this area.

As environmental pressures become more pressing and competition for resources raises the risk of intercommunal violence, it will be more important than ever that a clear framework for collaboration and conflict mitigation is in place. This is not only a question of sound land and water management, but also the protection of indigenous peoples' rights over their territory and the possibility for nomadic populations to continue to have access to land in order to graze their animals and preserve their way of life.

Palestine: 'Climate change is not just a natural phenomenon but a political one.'

A portrait of Abeer Butmeh, an environmental activist from Palestine. Romel De Vera

Abeer Butmeh is an environmental activist from Palestine and coordinator of the Palestinian Environmental NGO Network (PENGON). She talks to Muna Dajani about her work with PENGON and how she sees climate justice as central to the situation in the Occupied Palestinian Territories (OPT).

Working on environmental issues in the OPT, and on climate change campaigns in particular, might not seem like a priority, especially in the context of the Israeli occupation. However, it is relevant as it pertains to the everyday access to natural resources, and their use and control. After decades of precarious conditions related to military and resource exploitation, working on combating climate change and its impacts cannot be separated from politics. Climate change is therefore not just a natural phenomenon but a political one, exacerbating pre-existing injustice and inequality. The Israeli occupation exacerbates the climate risks facing Palestinians by denying them the right to manage their land and resources, making them more vulnerable to climate-related events.

In the OPT, climate change advocacy and activism take place on two fronts: the global and the local. We, as civil society organizations and individuals, participate in the United Nations Framework Convention on Climate Change (UNFCCC)'s Conference of the Parties (COP), as we see these as a useful platform to highlight the effects of climate change and raise awareness of the impact of the Israeli occupation. While the Palestinian Authority (PA)'s role and ability to implement adaptation policies remain restricted, it is important to be represented at such conferences as they provide a platform for awareness-raising and advocacy on how to tackle climate change under conditions of military occupation and resource exploitation. The PA's role in designing and implementing effective adaptation strategies is limited under such conditions – hence the need to work locally.

This is why we work on the Climate Justice campaign, which is an initiative to mainstream renewable energy through advocacy and lobbying. We believe energy transformation is critical for tackling climate change. Palestinians in the OPT are forced to depend on the infrastructure of the Israeli occupation for most of their electricity supply. Therefore, any climate justice advocacy must consider energy independence and sovereignty as its objective. At

'The Israeli occupation has now designated more than half of the agricultural land in the Jordan Valley as closed military zones. Consequently, Bedouin communities who depend heavily on pasture land and livestock have had to adapt to limited access to ever-shrinking areas and natural resources.'

PENGON we are working on many issues that target women in the field of renewable energy. Climate change work in the OPT has largely disregarded the role of women. Our work at PENGON has focused on revising the PA's energy strategy and relevant legislation to ensure gender is taken into account.

Our work also includes devising campaigns to confront controversial projects in which European countries are involved with Israel, with total disregard for the Israeli occupation and its practices, allowing for its normalization. One such campaign is against the underwater power cable known as the EuroAsia Interconnector, a project between Israel, Cyprus and Greece aimed at connecting the national grids of these countries. We participate in lobby tours in Europe to highlight how such endeavours are not only are detrimental for the environment, but also make European governments complicit in Israeli human rights violations and Israel's occupation of Palestinian land and resources. Locally, we work on lobbying and advocacy in order to mainstream climate change in the PA's

national strategy. Also, many initiatives such as Earth Hour, Fridays for Future and others are also organized locally by Palestinian youth and civil society.

The agricultural communities are the most vocal about the impacts of climate change, as their livelihoods have been transformed by a combination of Israeli occupation practices and climatic shifts. Farmers have had to devise adaptive measures to overcome these factors, such as crop variation, water-saving irrigation methods and the adoption of traditional approaches to agriculture. However, farmers realize the complexity of adopting such strategies and implementing them on the ground. The Israeli occupation has now designated more than half of the agricultural land in the Jordan Valley as closed military zones. Consequently, Bedouin communities who depend heavily on pasture land and livestock have had to adapt to limited access to ever-shrinking areas and natural resources. Relying on rainwater for their agriculture and animal husbandry means that they are highly vulnerable and at risk because of fluctuating rainfall and temperature change. The injustice is exposed when comparing their situation to that of Israeli settlers, who enjoy a reliable water supply and support of their agricultural production.

Such protracted injustice regarding the conditions of resource distribution, combined with the imminent threat of climate change impacts on Palestinian communities, means that climate change is framed as a justice issue in Palestine and not merely an issue of state-led legislation. This is why the role of women is at the heart of the Climate Justice campaign. Some areas in the West Bank, such as the Jordan Valley, are prime examples of the unjust and unequal impacts of climate change on the same geographical areas. While Palestinian farmers in villages such as Al Auja suffer from drought and water scarcity, the illegal Israeli settlements nearby enjoy access to water for their irrigated lands. We highlighted such unequal realities in 'From Another Side', an exhibition highlighting Israeli human rights violations in relation to the Palestinian environment. Using photos taken from the same location, one shot shows the reality of life in the Palestinian community, while the other shows the Israeli side in order to expose discrimination and injustice in resource distribution and access. We also focus on publishing reports and studies to highlight such realities

and even lobby for accountability for such actions in UN institutions and the European Commission. We are lobbying against the Europe–Israel gas pipeline. We also worked on the Stop Mekorot campaign (Mekorot is the Israeli water company), raising awareness about how this company is implementing water injustice by controlling Palestinian access and rights to use their water sources, and denying Palestinians access. These campaigns are connecting the local with the global and creating linkages beyond borders to expose how injustice can be resisted and transformed. The struggle over climate injustice is therefore a collective struggle that we as Palestinians need to fight collectively with our allies and counterparts all over the world.

Recognizing the intergenerational aspect of climate change also pushes us, as environmental institutions and practitioners, to consider the role of youth in addressing this climate crisis and transforming it into an opportunity for positive change. We run initiatives, such as the sustainable schools project, that aim to enhance the skills of young environmental activists and highlight their potential in mainstreaming and tackling climate change issues. The active involvement of youth in global events such as Earth Hour is also indicative of how climate change is a global concern that requires local action.

Yemen: As the civil war rages on, the island of Socotra battles with climate change

A local man looks at a canyon on the Dixsam plateau on the island of Socotra, Yemen. Alamy / *Robert Harding*

Socotra is an archipelago consisting of the islands of Socotra (also referred to as Soqotra), Abd al-Kuri, Samha, Darsa and the islets of Kal Farun and Sabuniya. Part of the Hadramawt governorate, it is situated in the Indian Ocean, south of the Gulf of Aden, around 250 kilometres off the tip of the Horn of Africa. Its unique biodiversity, including its famous dragon's blood tree, is due in part to its physical isolation: until relatively recently, Socotra was largely unreachable from Yemen during the entire monsoon season. It also hosts a wide variety of flora, fauna, reptiles, birds and other forms of wildlife that are endemic to the area.

Socotra's population is as unique as the archipelago's biosphere, and Socotris comprise a distinct ethnic group. Studies of Socotra's population point again towards its isolation from the rest of the Arabian Peninsula. According to the 2004 Census, Socotra's population totalled 42,842 inhabitants, although various sources cite around 60,000 at present. Socotris have their own language, an archaic yet living Afro-Asiatic and South Arabian language known as Socotri, that is only spoken on the archipelago and that includes a number of dialects. Though for centuries the inhabitants were Nestorian Christians, following the arrival of the Mehra sultanate on the island the inhabitants steadily Islamicized and today Socotris are almost entirely Muslim, split between Zaidis (an offshoot of Shi'a Islam), Sunni Shafi'is and smaller numbers of Ismailis on the archipelago. Socotra itself has remained largely undeveloped and acquired its first proper road only a few years ago.

Socotra has long been somewhat removed from developments on the Yemeni mainland. Following the takeover of Sana'a in 2014 by the Houthis, an armed group originating from Saada in the North, a coalition of Arab states led by Saudi Arabia launched a military campaign on Yemen in 2015, with the declared aim of restoring the internationally recognized government of President Abd-Rabbur Mansur Hadi. While the whole of Yemen has been ravaged by war since, Socotra, due to its natural isolation, was initially sheltered from it. However, later that year the islands were hit by two successive cyclones just a week apart – an unprecedented development that uprooted as much as a third of the island's population and devastated the local environment. These highly unusual events were blamed by researchers on a combination of environmental pressures, including – besides the effects of El Niño – climate change and air pollution. Fears that Socotra could find itself exposed to further extreme weather in future were sadly confirmed in 2018 when another cyclone hit, further devastating the island's limited infrastructure and leaving at least 19 people dead.

Mirroring these developments, the political situation for Socotra has also become more troubled as the United Arab Emirates has steadily established a presence on the island. While initially welcomed in 2015 when, in the midst of the destruction left by the cyclones, the country provided considerable humanitarian assistance to the population, since then its involvement has become more controversial. As one of the main actors in the Saudi-led coalition fighting in Yemen, the United Arab Emirates supports the local apparatus loyal to the Southern Transitional Council, a group that has frequently engaged in fighting with the Islah party, despite its ties to President Hadi. Tensions between the two have resulted in numerous clashes and the government of President Hadi, having previously supported the UAE's move into Socotra, has since accused it of effectively staging an occupation. As a result, Socotra, until then largely sheltered from the conflict raging on the mainland, has seen some of the dynamics of the conflict spreading to its shores. Local resentment of UAE and its increasing military footprint, as well as its apparent annexation of the island as a base, have resulted in protests on the streets. New factions have been formed, with some demonstrating in support of Yemen while others carry UAE flags.

In this context, Socotra's population must now recover from the trauma of its recent natural disasters, while political divisions on the island continue to increase. Just as they have played no part in the development of conflict on the mainland, so too the Socotri community has contributed little to climate change – and yet, like other communities on the frontline of global warming, they are now faced with its worst effects. With swathes of its wildlife devastated by the cyclones, development and climate change could further undermine Socotra's fragile ecosystem – a situation that has prompted the International Union for Conservation of Nature (IUCN) to recommend the island to be listed on the UN Educational, Scientific and Cultural Organization (UNESCO)'s List of World Heritage in Danger.

This is an edited version of the community entry in the profile of Yemen in MRG's online World Directory of Minorities and Indigenous Peoples. ▪

In 2015 the islands were hit by two successive cyclones just a week apart – an unprecedented development that uprooted as much as a third of the island's population and devastated the local environment.

Yemen: As the civil war rages on, the island of Socotra battles with climate change

www.minorityrights.org/trends2019

Find more case studies, multimedia stories and updated profiles of over 100 countries.

minority
rights
group
international

YEARS

Defending diversity since 1969